LIGHTS ON LIFE-PROBLEMS

LIGHTS ON LIFE-PROBLEMS

Sri Aurobindo's views on important life-problems,
compiled from his writings

by

Kishor Gandhi

SRI AUROBINDO ASHRAM
PONDICHERRY

First edition: First series 1950; Second series 1951
Second edition (combined) 1987
Third edition 2011
Third impression 2020

Rs 120
ISBN 978-81-7058-939-6

© Sri Aurobindo Ashram Trust 1950, 1951, 2011
Published by Sri Aurobindo Ashram Publication Department
Pondicherry 605 002
Web https://www.sabda.in

Printed at Sri Aurobindo Ashram Press, Pondicherry
PRINTED IN INDIA

COMPILER'S NOTE

Lights on Life-Problems originally appeared in the form of a series of instalments in the fortnightly review *Mother India,* since its beginning on 19 February 1949 till 27 January 1951. The proposal to run this series in *Mother India* was sanctioned by Sri Aurobindo himself. To make clear the object of this series a note was placed at the top of each of the earlier instalments. In the later instalments this note was substituted by a slightly altered note containing some revisions which Sri Aurobindo made in it. This revised note stood as follows:

> One of our chief aims will be to provide authentic guidance in regard to many important questions which arise in the minds of thoughtful persons all over the world. This cannot be better done than by considering these questions in the light of Sri Aurobindo's writings, because Sri Aurobindo is not merely a Master of Yoga in possession of the eternal spiritual Truths, but also a Guide and Helper of mankind in various spheres of life and thought. To bring home the light of this guidance and to make it directly applicable to the problems that present themselves to an observing intelligence, a series of questions of common interest along with precise answers directly taken from Sri Aurobindo's writings will regularly appear in these columns.

Each instalment of the series, consisting of questions framed by the compiler and answers to them taken from Sri Aurobindo's writings, was submitted to Sri Aurobindo for perusal and approval before it was published. Only the last instalment could not be seen by him because soon after it was submitted to him for approval he left his body on 5 December 1950. The Mother then told the compiler that she herself would see it. She read it and returned it to him with her approval. The publication of the series was then discontinued with the Mother's consent.

The references to Sri Aurobindo's books from which all the answers are taken are shown in the Appendix at the end of the book.

Compiler's Note

It should be noted that while seeing these instalments Sri Aurobindo himself made alterations in the text of some of the passages quoted from his works in the answers. Some of these alterations were of a minor nature but some others were quite extensive. For this reason the text of the passages quoted in some of the answers is not exactly similar to the original text in Sri Aurobido's works. Further details about the references are mentioned in the Appendix.

The First Edition of this book, containing the first 25 instalments of the series, which appeared in *Mother India* fortnightly from 19 February 1949 (Vol. I, No. 1) till 18 March 1950 (Vol. II, No. 3) and which dealt with various problems of general interest, was published with the approval of Sri Aurobindo and the Mother by Sri Aurobindo Circle, Bombay, in 1950 under the title, *Lights on Life-Problems,* First Series. A Second Series of this book containing the next 18 instalments, which appeared in *Mother India* from 1 April 1950 (Vol. II, No. 4) till 27 January 1951 (Vol. II, No. 24) and which dealt with problems relating to Art, Literature and Poetry, was published in a separate volume by the same publishers in 1951.

In the present Second Edition, published by Sri Aurobindo Ashram, these two Series are combined in one volume and are brought out in a new format.

The compiler is grateful to the Sri Aurobindo Ashram Trust for granting its kind permission to reproduce in this book passages from Sri Aurobindo's works.

FOREWORD TO THE FIRST EDITION

This series of *Lights on Life-Problems* has been appearing in the fortnightly review *Mother India,* since its inception in February 1949. It was started at the instance of its Managing Editor, Mr. Keshavdev Poddar, who wanted to make it a special object of that review to make available to the general public Sri Aurobindo's views on the various important problems of life which arise in the minds of thoughtful persons everywhere. Sri Aurobindo is now universally recognised as a Master Yogi and a supreme authority on all matters relating to spiritual knowledge and practice; but, though this is not generally known, he is no less an authority in the various spheres of secular life because he has at his command a profound, extensive and intimate knowledge of all types of human experience and a deeply sympathetic understanding of all human situations. Since the spiritual discipline, which he has himself practised and which he has enunciated for others, does not aim at a withdrawal from human life but at a radical and total transformation of it, and since that transformation is not possible without a decisive conquest of life's basic difficulties, he had to make it his constant concern to have as close a grip as possible on the endlessly complex and incalculably variable possibilities of human experience. The truth of human life is not evident on its apparent surface and one who wants truly to understand and effectively to master it has to probe its hidden depths. For this reason Sri Aurobindo had always a double task laid upon him for the realisation of his life-work; he had on the one hand to scale and conquer the utmost heights of the spirit and on the other hand to plunge into and master the inmost depths of life — without shunning any difficulty or recoiling from any danger — and to establish an effective link between these sundered poles of existence. The Roman dramatist's dictum "nihil humani alienum" is more true of him than of any other person in the history of the human race.

Sri Aurobindo's views on questions of spiritual knowledge and practice, as set forth by him in a systematic and exhaustive manner in a number of books, have been available to the public for the last two decades. His views on the many issues of man's life and thought

Foreword

in the secular field have not been, however, set forth in this manner. An attempt is therefore made in this series to make known his views on these issues in as definite a manner as possible. The catechetic method has been adopted for this purpose as it seemed best suited to bring home in a direct and precise manner the unfailing light of Sri Aurobindo's profound wisdom on the various important life-problems that present themselves to an observing intelligence. The questions in each series have been so framed as to give a precise formulation to the several aspects of each of these problems and the answers to them have been supplied by directly reproducing those passages from Sri Aurobindo's works which provide the right solution of these questions. It has not always been possible to deal exclusively with the secular questions and to leave out the spiritual topics altogether, for in reality there is no clear-cut line of demarcation between the two fields especially in Sri Aurobindo's vision which unrelentingly strives for their harmonious realignment and true integration.

Endless gratitude is due to Sri Aurobindo for not only sanctioning the proposal to run this series but also for sparing his extremely valuable time to see and approve each instalment of it before publication.

24 April 1950   KISHOR GANDHI

CONTENTS

FIRST SERIES

I	Predictions and Prophecies — Fate and Karma	...	3
II	Search for Happiness	...	6
III	Possibilities of Love	...	9
IV	Love and Sex	...	13
V	Transformation of Sex-Energy	...	18
VI	The Role of Religion	...	22
VII	Religion and Reason	...	27
VIII	Superstitions — Popular Beliefs — Occultism	...	33
IX	Communications with the Dead — Supernatural Phenomena	...	38
X	The Problem of Good and Evil (I)	...	43
XI	The Problem of Good and Evil (2)	...	48
XII	The Problem of Good and Evil (3)	...	53
XIII	The Law of Karma	...	58
XIV	Karma and Free-Will	...	63
XV	Karma and Rebirth	...	68
XVI	Karma and Justice	...	74
XVII	Karma and Morality	...	81
XVIII	The Pursuit of Knowledge	...	86
XIX	Subjectivism and Objectivism (1)	...	92
XX	Subjectivism and Objectivism (2)	...	96
XXI	Subjectivism and Objectivism (3)	...	101
XXII	Subjectivism and Objectivism (4)	...	106
XXIII	Subjectivism and Objectivism (5)	...	112
XXIV	Materialism (1)	...	115
XXV	Materialism (2)	...	122

SECOND SERIES

I	Art for Art's Sake	...	131
II	Intellectual Thought, Philosophy and Poetry	...	137
III	Science, Philosophy, Religion and Poetry	...	141
IV	Poetry and Life	...	147

Contents

V	Realism in Art and Poetry	...	151
VI	Decadence in Modern Art and Literature	...	158
VII	Surrealist Art and Poetry (1)	...	163
VIII	Surrealist Art and Poetry (2)	...	167
IX	Art and the Common Man — Subjective Element in Appreciation of Art	...	173
X	Influence of Tradition and Environment on Poetic Creation	...	177
XI	Western Misunderstanding of Indian Art	...	182
XII	Ancient Indian Architecture (1)	...	188
XIII	Ancient Indian Architecture (2)	...	194
XIV	Ancient Indian Sculpture	...	199
XV	Ancient Indian Painting	...	205
XVI	Art and Morality	...	211
XVII	Art and National Character — Poetry, Music and Art	...	216
XVIII	Intellectual and Spiritual Value of Art	...	221
Appendix		...	225

First Series

Sri Aurobindo

I

PREDICTIONS AND PROPHECIES — FATE AND KARMA

Is it possible to predict future events? Is there such a thing as destiny?

What is evident is that in the course of events there is an element of the predictable, predictable accurately in detail as well as in large points. But it is not true that all is predictable or that destiny is the sole governing factor of existence. Neither is it true that there is a complete free will. The popular view of the matter that all is destiny or else all is free will is quite summary and inconclusive.

How is it that so many of Cheiro's prophecies have come true?

One cannot put great confidence in Cheiro's ideas and prophecies — some have come true but most have gone wrong; in fact the number of his prophecies that have failed to come off is rather staggering. So it is not possible to conclude from Cheiro's evidence that everything is predetermined or that an unchangeable destiny governs everything and everyone.

It is a known fact that a large number of astrological predictions have come true. Does this not prove that the stars rule our destiny?

If we take all astrological predictions together, we have to admit that quite a mass of them have come true. But it does not follow that the stars rule our destiny. The stars merely record a destiny that has been already formed. They are a hieroglyph, not a Force, — or if their action constitutes a force, it is a transmitting energy, not an originating Power. Someone is there who has determined or something is there which is Fate, let us say; the stars are only indicators.

How is it that in some cases astrological predictions fulfil themselves accurately up to a certain age and then no more come true? In case of prophecies also some come true to the letter, others do not — they half fulfil or misfire entirely.

Yes, that happens quite often, but it does not follow that the power of prediction is unreal or that the accurate predictions can be all explained by probability, chance or coincidence. The nature and number of those that cannot is too great. The variability of fulfilment may be explained either by an imperfect power in the prophet sometimes active, sometimes failing or by the fact that things are predictable in part only, they are determined in part only or else they are determined by different factors or lines of power, different series of potentials and actuals. So long as one is in touch with one line one predicts accurately, otherwise not — or if the lines of power change, one's prophecy also goes off the rails. All the same, one may say, there must be, if things are predictable at all, some power or plane through which or on which all is foreseeable; if there is a divine Omniscience and Omnipotence, it must be so.

Is human will entirely helpless before Fate or destiny?

The astrologers themselves say that there are two forces, *daiva* and *puruṣakāra*, Fate and individual energy, and individual energy can modify and even frustrate Fate. Even what is determined by Fate has to be worked out, actually is worked out by a play of forces and in this play there is no absolute rigidity discoverable. Personal will or endeavour is one of those forces. Napoleon when asked why he believed in Fate, yet was always planning and acting, answered, "Because it is fated that I should work and plan"; in other words, his planning and acting were part of Fate, contributed to the results Fate had in view.

What is the explanation of Fate?

The Indian explanation of Fate is Karma. We ourselves are our own Fate through our actions, but the Fate created by us binds us, for what we have sown we must reap in this life or another.

Whatever may have been our past actions, cannot our present will determine to some extent the course of future happenings?

Certainly it can, because we are creating our Fate for the future even while undergoing old Fate from the past in the present. That gives a meaning to our will and action and does not, as European critics wrongly believe, constitute a rigid and sterilising fatalism.

Are we completely bound to undergo the results of our past Karma? Cannot our present will modify or prevent the consequences of our past actions in the present?

It is not impossible that our present will and action can annul or modify the past Karma; it is only certain strong effects called *utkata karma* that are non-modifiable. The achievement of spiritual consciousness, for example, can annul or give the power to annul past Karma; for then we enter into union with the cosmic or transcendent Divine Will which has the power to annul what it had created, break the narrow fixed lines of Karma and make possible a more plastic freedom and wideness. Neither Karma nor Astrology therefore points to a rigid and for ever immutable Fate.

II

SEARCH FOR HAPPINESS

It is said that the motive power behind all the actions and endeavours of men is the search for happiness. Is this true?

That is an easily made psychological proposition which can exist only by ignoring facts. If you say that it is the Ananda behind the veil which makes one act as a moving power, not as a "motive", that may be so, but that is a metaphysical, not a psychological generalisation. When a communist faces torture in a Nazi concentration camp, he is not doing it for the sake of Ananda or happiness, but for something else which makes him indifferent to Ananda or happiness or else compels him to face the loss of these things and even their very reverse, however painful it may be.

But evidently most people are after happiness and make it the aim of their life?

To say that all human beings are always wanting happiness untainted with sorrow is far too sweeping a generalisation. What can safely be admitted is that it is one very strong strain in human nature. But there are many men who are not after happiness and do not believe it is the true aim of life. And mark that it is the human physical consciousness only that seeks after happiness. The human vital tends rather to reject a happiness untained by sorrow and to find it a monotonous boring condition. Even if it accepts it, after a time it kicks over the traces and goes to some new painful or risky adventure. The higher vital is ready to sacrifice happiness in order to satisfy its passions, search for power, ambition, fame or any other motive. If you say it is because of the happiness power, fame, etc, give, that again is not universally true. Power can give anything else, but not happiness; it is something in its very nature arduous and full of difficulty to get, to keep or to use — speaking of course of power in the ordinary sense. A man may know he can never have fame in this life, but yet work in the hope of posthumous fame or on the chance of it. He may know that the satisfaction of his passion will bring him everything rather than happiness — suffering, torture, destruction — yet he will follow his impulse. So also the mind as well as the larger vital is not bound by the pursuit of happiness. It can seek Truth rather or the victory of a cause. To reduce all into a single hard construction seems to be very poor psychology. Neither Nature nor the vast Spirit in things is so limited and one-tracked as that.

Some say that even the wicked, the criminals, etc. sin because they are trying to find the self's happiness in the sins they commit. Is this true?

This is really a very summary and misleading criminal psychology. To say that a Paris crook or Apache steals, swindles, murders for the happiness of stealing, swindling, murdering, is a little startling. He does it for quite other reasons; he does it as his *métier* just as a doctor does his medical work. Can it always be said that the doctor does his work because of the happiness he finds in it?

Why is it so difficult to overcome unhappiness and suffering?

It is because something in the human vital clings to suffering and almost needs it as part of the drama of life. The external consciousness — the physical mind and consciousness of man — hates its own suffering and if left to itself dislikes also to see others suffer. But if we go deep enough we shall find that there is something in the vital which likes suffering and clings to it for the sake of the drama. It is something below the surface, but it is strong, almost universal in human nature and difficult to eradicate unless one recognises it and gets inwardly away from it. The mind and the physical of man do not like suffering, for if they did, it would not be suffering any longer, but this thing in the vital wants it in order to give a spice to life. It is the reason, for example, why constant depressions can go on returning and returning even though the mind longs to get rid of them, because this in the vital responds, goes on repeating the same movement like a gramophone as soon as it is got going and insists on turning the whole round of the oft-repeated record. It does not really depend on the reasons which the vital gives for starting off the round; these are often of the most trivial character and wholly insufficient to justify it. It is only by a strong will to detach oneself, not to justify, to reject, not to welcome, that one can in the end get rid of this most troublesome and dangerous streak in human nature. In speaking therefore of the vital comedy, of the vital drama, we are speaking from a psychological knowledge which does not end with the surface of things but looks at these hidden movements. It is impossible to deal with things effectively and radically if we confine ourselves to their surface view only.

III

POSSIBILITIES OF LOVE

Anatole France says: "One can do no wrong when one really loves, but sensual passion is made up of hatred, egoism and wrath as much as love." But is not love itself as it exists between human beings mostly egoistic in character?

Yes, the human feeling of love is always either based on or strongly mixed with ego, — that is why it cannot be pure. It is said in the Upanishad, "One does not love the wife for the sake of the wife, but for one's self's sake one loves the wife." There is usually a hope of return, of benefit or advantage of some kind, or of certain pleasures and gratifications, mental, vital or physical that the loved can give. Remove these things and the love very soon sinks, diminishes or turns into anger, reproach, indifference or even hatred. The vital element in human love is especially dominated by ego and desire. It is full of craving and demand; its continuance depends upon the satisfaction of its demands. If it does not get what it craves or even imagines that it is not being treated as it deserves — for it is full of imaginations, misunderstandings, jealousies, misinterpretations — it at once turns to sorrow, wounded feeling, anger, all kinds of disorder, finally cessation and departure. A love of this kind is only a source of suffering, trouble, disappointment, disillusion and disunion and in its very nature ephemeral and unreliable.

Is human love always of this kind? Can it not take a purer and nobler form?

Human love is usually a mixture of ignorance, attachment, passion and desire but it can take an unselfish, noble and pure form and expression if it is touched by the psychic. There is in the highest or deepest kind of love this psychic element which comes from the inmost heart and soul. It is a kind of inner union or self-giving or at least a seeking for that, a tie or an urge independent of other conditions or elements, existing for its own sake and not for any mental, vital or physical pleasure, satisfaction, interest or habit. But usually the psychic element in human love, even when present, is not left pure; it is so much mixed, overloaded and hidden under the other elements that it gets little chance of fulfilling itself or achieving its own natural purity and fullness. What is called love is therefore sometimes one thing, sometimes another, most often a confused mixture.

The psychic love may be purer than the vital love but does it not lack the flaming intensity and the warm glow of the vital love which so powerfully attract the human heart?

It is a mistake to think that the vital alone has warmth and the psychic is something frigid without any flame in it. Psychic love can have a warmth and a flame as intense and more intense than the vital; only it is a pure fire, not dependent on the satisfaction of ego-desire or on the eating up of the fuel it embraces. It is a white flame, not a red one; but white heat is not inferior to the red variety in its ardour. It is true that the psychic love does not usually get its full play in human relations and human nature; it finds the fullness of its fire and ecstasy more easily when it is lifted towards the Divine. In the human relation the psychic love gets mixed up with other elements which seek at once to use it and overshadow it. It gets an outlet for its own full intensities only at rare moments. Otherwise it comes in only as an element, but even so it contributes all the higher things in a love fundamentally vital — all the finer sweetness, tenderness, fidelity, self-giving, self-sacrifice, reachings of soul to soul, idealising sublimations that lift up human love beyond itself, come from the psychic. If it could dominate and govern and transmute the other elements — mental, vital, physical — of human love, then love could be on the earth some reflection or preparation of the real thing, an integral union of the soul and its instruments in a dual life. But even some imperfect appearance of that is rare.

In the vital love itself are there no elements akin to the psychic love? Is it all made up of ego and craving?

There are in the vital itself two kinds of love, — one full of joy and confidence and abandon, generous, unbargaining, ungrudging and very absolute in its dedication and this is akin to the psychic love. But there is another way of vital love which is the usual way of human nature which is made up of ego and desire and which is mostly a cause of trouble and suffering. It neither satisfies nor lasts.

Why is human vital love so evanescent?

It is because it is a passion which Nature has thrown in in order to serve a temporary purpose; it is good enough therefore for a temporary purpose and its normal tendency is to wane when it has sufficiently served Nature's purpose. In mankind, as man is a more complex being, she calls in the aid of imagination and idealism to help her push, gives a sense of ardour, of beauty and fire and glory, but all that wanes after a time. It cannot last because it is all a borrowed light and power, borrowed in the sense of being a reflection caught from something beyond and not native to the reflecting vital medium which imagination uses for the purpose. Moreover, nothing lasts in the mind and vital, all is a flux there. The one thing that endures is the soul, the spirit. Therefore love can last or satisfy only if it bases itself on the soul and spirit, if it has its roots there. But that means living no longer in the vital but in the soul and spirit.

How can vital love get liberation from its usual insufficiencies and achieve the fulfilment of its secret urge?

Like the mind and the physical, the vital is properly an instrument for the soul and spirit; when it works for itself it produces ignorant and imperfect results, but if it can be made into a conscious instrument of the psychic and the spirit, then it gets its own divine fulfilment; that is the idea contained in what is called transformation in Yoga.

According to McTaggart, "Love is authentic and justifies itself completely whether its cause be great or trivial." How far is this true of the human relationships of love?

What McTaggart says is not often true in human practice; for there the destiny of love and its justification depend very much as a rule (though not always) on the nature of the cause or object. For if the object of love is trivial in the sense of its being an inadequate instrument for the dynamic realisation of the sense of oneness which McTaggart says is the essence of love, then love is likely to be baulked of its fulfilment. Unless, of course, it is satisfied with existing, with spending itself in its own fundamental way on the loved without expecting any return for its self-expenditure, any mutual unification. Still, of love in its essence the statement may be true.

What is the nature of love in its essence and origin?

Love at its origin is a self-existent force, an absolute, a transcendent, which does not depend upon the objects — it depends only on itself or only on the Divine; for it is a self-existent power of the Divine. If it were not self-existent, it would hardly be independent of the nature or reaction of its objects. It is partly what is meant when we speak of transcendent Love — though this is only one aspect of its transcendence. That self-existent transcendent Love spreading itself over all, turning everywhere to contain, embrace, unite, help, upraise towards love and bliss and oneness, becomes cosmic divine Love; intensely fixing itself on one or other to find itself, to achieve a dynamic unification or to reach here towards the union of the soul with the Divine, it becomes the individual divine Love. But there are unhappily its diminutions in the human mind, human vital, human physical; there the divine essence of Love easily becomes mixed with counterfeits, dimmed, concealed or lost in the twisted movements born of division and ignorance.

IV

LOVE AND SEX

Schopenhauer, the great German philosopher, considers love to be an illusion. According to him, when a youth and a girl fall in each other's arms in the ecstasy of love they imagine that they are seeking their own happiness, but it is really not so. They are only deluded by the impersonal will of the race into the belief that they are seeking a personal end in order that they may be induced to effect a far greater impersonal end — the creation of the race. Love is thus, to Schopenhauer, an unconscious sacrifice made by the lovers to Nature's ends. How far is this view true?

It is perfectly true, not only of love as Schopenhauer means it, but of all human activities and movements of Nature. All movements are in the mass movements of Nature's cosmic forces, they are movements of universal Nature. The individual receives something of them, a wave or pressure of some cosmic force, and is driven by it; he thinks it is his own, generated in himself separately, but it is not so; it is part of a general movement which works just in the same way in others. Sex, for instance, is a movement of general Nature seeking for its play and it uses this or that one — a man vitally or physically "in love", as it is called, with a woman is simply repeating and satisfying the world-movement of sex; if it had not been that woman, it would have been another; he is simply an instrument in Nature's machinery, it is not an independent movement. So it is with anger and other Nature-motives. An executive cosmic force shapes us and dictates through our temperament and environment and mentality so shaped, through our individualised formulation of the cosmic energies, our actions and their results. Truly, we do not think, will or act but thought occurs in us, will occurs in us, impulse and act occurs in us; our ego-sense gathers around itself, refers to itself all this flow of natural activities. It is Cosmic Force, it is Nature that forms the thought, imposes the will, imparts the impulse. Our body, mind and ego are a wave of that sea of force in action and do not govern it, but by it are governed and directed.

What purpose does Cosmic Nature work out through the action of the universal sex-energy in the individual?

The terrestrial sex-movement is a utilisation by Nature of the fundamental physical energy for purposes of procreation and the sex-energy is in its real nature a fundamental energy of life. In the economy of the material creation in the Ignorance the action of the animal sex-energy is thus a device for a particular purpose. It is a great power with two components in its physical basis, one meant for procreation and the process necessary for it, the other for feeding the general energies of the body, mind and vital, — also of the spiritual energies of the body. The sex-energy is thus the support in the body of all the spiritual, mental, vital and physical forces of the nature. Its misuse, therefore, turns to disorder and disintegration of the energies and powers of life.

Why has the sex-impulse so powerful a grip over human nature? Why is it difficult to get free of its hold even when its indulgence brings a reaction of disgust?

It is because the sex-impulse is the greatest force on the vital plane. The thrill which accompanies it is a very gross distortion and degradation of the divine Ananda. The pleasure attached to it is the lure by which Nature makes the vital consent to this otherwise unpleasing process. There are quite a number of persons who experience a recoil of disgust after the sexual act and repulsion from the partner in it because of the disgust, but they return to it when the disgust has worn off for the sake of the lure.

It is a common belief that sex-desire is stronger in men than in women. What is the truth in this belief?

There is no universal rule. Women can be as sexual as men or more. But there are numbers of women who dislike sex and there are very few men. One Shukdev in a million, but many Dianas and Pallas Athenes. The virgin is really a feminine conception; men are repelled by the idea of eternal virginity. Many women would remain without any wakening of the sexual instinct if men did not thrust it on them and that cannot be said of many, perhaps of any man. But there is another side to the picture. Women are perhaps less physically sexual than men on the whole, — but what about vital sexuality? the instinct of possessing and being possessed etc., etc.?

What is the distinction between physical love and vital love?

The two are not the same. It is possible for the vital to desire a woman for various vital reasons without love — in order to satisfy the instinct of domination or possession, in order to draw in the vital forces of a woman so as to feed one's own vital, for the exchange of vital forces, to satisfy vanity, the hunter's instinct of the chase, etc., etc. (This is from the man's viewpoint, but the woman also has her vital motives.) This is often called love, but it is only vital desire, a kind of lust. If, however, the emotions of the heart are awakened, then it becomes vital love — a mixed affair with any or all of these vital motives, strong, but still vital love.

But the physical love is different from this. It is the attraction of beauty, the physical sex appeal or anything else of the kind awakening the emotions of the heart. If that does not happen, then the physical need is all and that is sheer lust, nothing more. But physical love without lust is possible.

Love is really a function of the heart; so how can there be such a thing as mental love?

Why not? The mind is the seat of thought and perception, the heart is the seat of love, the vital of desire — but how does that prevent the existence of mental love? As the mind can be invaded by the feelings of the emotional or the vital, so the heart too can be dominated by the mind and moved by mental forces. Thus there can be a mental love. It arises from the attempt to find one's ideal in another or from some strong mental passion of admiration and wonder or from the mind's seeking for a comrade, a complement and fulfiller of one's nature, a *sahadharmī*, a guide and helper, a leader and master or from a hundred other mental motives. By itself that does not amount to love, though often it is so ardent as to be hardly distinguishable from it and may even push to sacrifice of life, entire self-giving, etc., etc. But when it awakes the emotions of the heart, then it may lead to a very powerful love which is yet mental in its root and dominant character. Ordinarily, however, it is the mind and vital together which combine.

Most of the modern psychologists hold the view that love between man and woman cannot exist without sexual desire and some even maintain that love is nothing but sex. Can there not be an ardent relation of love without sex at all coming in?

It is an ignorant psychology that reduces everything to the sex-motive and the sex-impulse. Though the sex-desire does usually enter in the intimate love relationships between men and women, it cannot be said that it is invariably so. As said before, there are a number of women who can love with the mind, the psychic, the vital (heart), but they shrink from a touch on the body and even when that goes, the physical act remains abhorrent to them. They may yield under pressure, but it does not reconcile them to the act which always seems to them animal and degrading. Love of a strong mental and vital character can exist along with a disinclination or positive dislike for the physical act and its accompaniments. No doubt, if the man presses, the woman is likely to yield, but it is *contre coeur,* as they say, against her feelings and her deepest instincts. Women know this, but men seem to find it hard to believe; but it is perfectly true.

The modern psychologists consider sex to be a natural human instinct, a necessity like food and sleep and an absence of this desire would be regarded by them as an abnormal condition. Is this true?

Abnormal is a word which you can stick on anything that is not quite cheap or ordinary. In that way genius is abnormal, so is spirituality, so is the attempt to live by high ideals. The tendency to physical chastity in women is not abnormal, it is fairly common and includes a very high feminine type.

V

TRANSFORMATION OF SEX-ENERGY

Balzac, the famous French novelist, was of the opinion that indulgence in sex greatly hampers the high type of mental activity. According to him, "The man of genius is frigid. When he tries to lead both lives, the intellectual life and the love life, the man of genius dies, as Raphael died and Lord Byron." So also Havelock Ellis, recognised as the world's greatest authority on sex, maintains that to increase artistic and mental capacity and force it is necessary to restrain sexual activity. "The brain and the sexual organs," he says, "are yet the great rivals in using up bodily energy, and there is an antagonism between extreme brain vigour and extreme sexual vigour, even though they may sometimes both appear at different periods in the same individual." We find this evidenced in the life of some great masters of art like Beethoven and Mozart, in whose life sexual indulgence played a much smaller part than in the life of an average man. This would seem to imply that it is necessary to conserve sexual energy for the energisation and intensification of higher intellectual and aesthetic life. How far is this view justifiable?

That is correct — the sex-energy can be controlled and diverted from the sex-purpose and used for aesthetic and artistic or other creation and productiveness or preserved for heightening of the intellectual or other energies. Entirely controlled it can be turned into a force of spiritual energy also. This was well known in ancient India and was described as the conversion of *retas* into *ojas* by Brahmacharya. *Retas* the sex-fluid, consists of two elements, one meant for sex-purposes, the other as a basis of general energy, and if the sex-action is not indulged and the sex-fluid is prevented from being spent away, it turns into *ojas*. The whole theory of Brahmacharya is based upon that by the Yogis. The European scientists generally pooh-

poohed the idea, but now they are beginning to discover the same fact for themselves.

What is the process by which retas is transformed into ojas?

The fundamental physical unit is the *retas*, in which the *tejas*, the heat and light and electricity in a man, is involved and hidden. All energy is thus latent in the *retas*. This energy may be either expended physically or conserved. All passion, lust, desire wastes the energy by pouring it, either in the gross form or a sublimated subtle form, out of the body. On the other hand, all self-control conserves the energies in the *retas,* and conservation always brings with it increase. But the needs of the physical body are limited and the excess of energy must create a surplus which has to turn itself to some use other than the physical. According to the ancient theory, *retas* is *jala* or water, full of light and heat and electricity, in one word *tejas*. The excess of the *retas* turns first into heat or *tapas* which stimulates the whole system, and it is for this reason that all forms of self-control and austerity are called *tapas* or *tapasyā*, because they generate the heat or stimulus which is a source of powerful action and success; secondly, it turns to *tejas* proper, the light, the energy which is at the source of all knowledge; thirdly, it turns to *vidyut* or electricity, which is at the basis of all forceful action whether intellectual or physical. In the *vidyut* again is involved the *ojas*, or *prāṇa śakti,* the primal energy which proceeds from ether. The *retas*, refining from *jala* to *tapas, tejas,* and *vidyut* and from *vidyut* to *ojas*, fills the system with physical strength, energy and brain-power and in its last form of *ojas* rises to the brain and informs it with that primal energy which is the most refined form of matter and nearest to spirit. It is *ojas* that creates a spiritual force or *vīrya*, by which a man attains to spiritual knowledge, spiritual love and faith, spiritual strength. It follows that the more we can by Brahmacharya increase the store of *tapas, tejas, vidyut* and *ojas*, the more we shall fill ourselves with utter energy for the works of the body, heart, mind and spirit.

> *Many eminent psychologists, doctors and thinkers believe that complete sexual abstinence is dangerous and may lead to serious nervous trouble and even mental derangement. They maintain that the new form of energy produced from the sublimation of sexual energy may be harmful and may lead to perversities and morbidities. René Guyon, for example, points out: "When the libido is repressed, when its impetus is crushed back, it is forced to find an outlet by some other route.... But this compensation is not necessarily useful, superior and worthy of admiration. It can just as well be harmful and destructive." How far is this true?*

It is a fact that sex suppressed in outward action but indulged in other ways may lead to disorders of the system and brain troubles. That is the root of the medical theory which discourages sexual abstinence. But these things happen only when there is either secret indulgence of a perverse kind replacing the normal sexual activity or else an indulgence of it in a kind of subtle vital way by imagination or by an invisible vital interchange of an occult kind; harm never occurs when there is true effort at mastery and abstinence. It is now held by many medical men in Europe that sexual abstinence, *if it is genuine* is beneficial.

> *The Freudian system of psycho-analysis has attributed a large number of physical and mental disorders to suppressed sexual desire. To what extent are the assertions of this system true?*

The psycho-analysis of Freud takes up a certain part, the darkest, the most perilous, the unhealthiest part of the nature, the lower vital subconscious layer, isolates some of its most morbid phenomena and attributes to it an action out of all proportion to its true role in the nature. Modern psychology is an infant science, at once rash, fumbling and crude. As in all infant sciences, the universal habit of the human mind — to take a partial or local truth, generalise it unduly and try to explain a whole field of Nature in its narrow terms — runs riot here. Moreover, the exaggeration of the importance of suppressed sexual complexes is a dangerous falsehood and it can have a nasty influence and tend to make the mind and vital more and not less fundamentally impure than before.

VI

THE ROLE OF RELIGION

In modern times, especially in Europe, the place of religion in life has not only been very much minimised and restricted but often religion has been violently attacked as a force making for retardation, oppression, superstition and ignorance. This revolt against religion has sought to keep science, philosophy and art, politics and practical life and even ethics entirely immune to the influence of religion and in its extreme form has tried to destroy religion altogether. To what extent is this indictment against religion justified?

This aggressive indictment against religion in modern times has much to justify it, not in its conclusion but in its premise, — not that religion in itself must always be, but that historically and as a matter of fact the accredited religions and their hierarchs and exponents have too often been a force for retardation, have too often thrown their weight on the side of darkness, oppression and ignorance, and that it has needed a denial, a revolt of the oppressed human mind and heart to correct these errors and set religion right. Though we need not lay a too excessive stress on the superstitions, aberrations, violences, crimes even, which Churches and cults and creeds have favoured, admitted, sanctioned, supported or exploited for their own benefit, we have to note the fact that such a thing was possible.

What is the explanation of so much evil perpetrated in the name of religion?

The root of this evil is not in true religion itself, but in our ignorant human confusion of religion with a particular creed, sect, cult, religious society or Church. The human tendency to this error is exremely strong and the whole root of the historic insufficiency of religion as a guide and control of human society

The Role of Religion   23

lies in this tendency. Churches and creeds have, for exmple, stood violently in the way of philosophy and science, burned a Giordano Bruno, imprisoned a Galileo, and so generally misconducted themselves in this matter that philosophy and science had in self-defence to turn upon religion and rend her to pieces in order to get a free field for their legitimate development; and this because men in the passion and darkness of their vital nature had chosen to think that religion was bound up with certain fixed intellectual conceptions about God and the world which could not stand scrutiny, and therefore scrutiny had to be put down by fire and sword; scientific and philosophical truth had to be denied in order that religious error might survive. We see too that a narrow religious spirit often oppresses and impoverishes the joy and beauty of life, either from an intolerant asceticism or, as the Puritans attempted it, because they could not see that religious austerity is not the whole of religion, though it may be an important side of it, is not the sole ethico-religious approach to God, since love, charity, gentleness, tolerance, kindliness are also and even more divine, and they forgot or never knew that God is love and beauty as well as purity. In politics religion has often thrown itself on the side of power and resisted the coming of larger political ideals, because it was itself, in the form of a Church, supported by power and because it confused religion with the Church, or because it stood for a false theocracy, forgetting that true theocracy is the kingdom of God in man and not the kingdom of a Pope, a priesthood or a sacerdotal class. So too it has often supported a rigid and outworn social system, because it thought its own life bound up with social forms with which it happened to have been associated during a long portion of its own history and erroneously concluded that even a necessary change there would be a violation of religion and a danger to its existence. As if so mighty and inward a power as the religious spirit in man could be destroyed by anything so small as the change of a social form or so outward as a social readjustment! This error in its many shapes has been the great weakness of religion as practised in the past and the opportunity and justification for the revolt of the intelligence, the aesthetic sense, the social and political idealism, even the ethical spirit of the human being against what should have been its own highest tendency and law.

In ancient times religion was the most dominant thing in man's life and governed all his individual and social activities. The modern age, on the contrary, considers religion as the enemy of progress and has tried to banish it from life. How are these two divergent attitudes to be reconciled?

Both the attitudes rest upon a certain strong justification and their quarrel is due to misunderstanding. It is true in a sense that religion should be the dominant thing in life, its light and law, but religion as it should be and is in its inner nature, its fundamental law of being, a seeking after God, the cult of spirituality, the opening of the deepest life of the soul to the indwelling Godhead, the eternal Omnipresence; on the other hand, it is true that religion when it identifies itself only with a creed, a cult, a Church, a system of ceremonial forms, may well become a retarding force and there may therefore arise a necessity for the human spirit to reject its control over the varied activities of life.

But by spirituality religion often means something remote from earthly life, different from it, hostile to it. The spirit then becomes something aloof which man can reach only by throwing away the life or by persistently discouraging, mortifying and killing it. If that be the true sense of religion, how can it have any positive message for human society in its effort or aspiration for progress or perfection in its own sphere? If religion discourages life and holds out no hope to it, how can it be its true law and guide?

All such religious pessimistic notions of life which have weighed so heavily on man's mind both in the East and the West in the past are a denial of the fullness and power of the Spirit, an impatience with the ways of God in the world, an insufficient faith in the divine Wisdom and Will which created the world and for ever guide it. All pessimism admits a wrong notion about that supreme Wisdom and Power and therefore cannot itself be the supreme wisdom and power of the spirit to which the world can look for guidance and for the uplifting of its whole life towards the Divine.

In spirituality, then, understood in this true and complete sense, we must seek for the directing light and the harmonising law, and in religion only in proportion as it identifies itself with this spirituality. So long as it falls short of this, it is one human activity and power among others, and, even if it be considered the most important and the most powerful, it cannot wholly guide the others. If it seeks always to fix them into the limits of a creed, an unchangeable law, a particular system, it must be prepared to see them revolting from its control; for although they may accept this impress for a time and greatly profit by it, in the end they must move by the law of their being towards a freer and an untrammelled movement. Spirituality respects the freedom of the human soul because it is itself fulfilled by freedom; and the deepest meaning of freedom is the power to expand and grow towards perfection by the law of one's own nature, *dharma*. This liberty it will give to all the fundamental parts of our being. It will give that freedom to philosophy and science which ancient Indian religion gave, — freedom even to deny the spirit, if they will, — as a result of which philosophy and science never felt in ancient India any necessity of divorcing themselves from religion, but grew rather into it and under its light. It will give the same freedom to man's seeking for political and social perfection and to all his other powers and aspirations. Only it will be vigilant to illuminate them so that they may grow into the light and law of the spirit, not by suppression and restriction, but by a self-searching, self-controlled expansion and a many-sided finding of their greatest, highest and deepest potentialities. For all these are potentialities of the spirit.

> *Mahatma Gandhi, commenting on Dr. Ambedkar's advocacy of change of religion stated, "But religion is not like a house or a cloak which can be changed at will. It is more an integral part of one's self than of one's body. Religion is the tie that binds one to one's creator, and while the body perishes as it has to, religion persists even after that." Is there not some exaggeration in this statement?*

If it is meant by the statement that the form of religion is something permanent and unchangeable, then that cannot be accepted. But if religion here means one's way of communion with the Divine, then it is true that that is something belonging to the inner being and cannot be changed like a house or a cloak for the sake of some personal, social or worldly convenience. If a change is to be made, it can only be for an inner spiritual reason, because of some development from within. No one can be bound to any form of religion or any particular creed or system, but if he changes the one he has accepted for another, for external reasons, that means he has inwardly no religion at all and both his old and his new religion are only an empty formula. At bottom that is, I suppose, what the statement drives at. Preference for a different approach to the Truth or the desire of inner spiritual self-expression are not the motives of the recommendation of change to which objection is made here; — the object proposed is an enhancement of social status and consideration which is no more a spiritual motive than conversion for the sake of money or marriage. If a man has no religion in himself, he can change his credal profession for any motive; if he has, he cannot; he can only change it in response to an inner spiritual need. If a man has *bhakti* for the Divine in the form of Krishna, he can't very well say, "I will scrap Krishna for Christ, so that I may become socially respectable."

VII

RELIGION AND REASON

The extremist type of modern mind has dismissed religion altogether by branding it as a mass of superstitious nonsense, but a more moderate type of that mind has taken a less intolerant attitude to it by not banishing it entirely but by creating what it calls a rational religion. Is this rational religion of any value?

This more moderate attitude of the rational mind to religion is as shallow, presumptuous and erroneous as the thoroughgoing extremist attitude. Its attempts to explain religion have resulted in the compilation of an immense mass of amazingly ingenious perversions, such as certain pseudo-scientific attempts to form a comparative Science of Religion. It has built up in the approved modern style immense façades of theory with stray bricks of misunderstood facts for their material. Its mild condonations of religion have led to superficial phases of thought which have passed quickly away and left no trace behind them. Its efforts at the creation of a rational religion, perfectly well-intentioned, but helpless and unconvincing, have had no appreciable effect and have failed like a dispersing cloud, *chinnābhramiva naśyati*. A purely rational religion could only be a cold and bare Deism, and such attempts have always failed to achieve vitality and permanence; for they act contrary to the *dharma*, the natural law and the spirit of religion.

Has religion then nothing to do with reason?

The deepest heart, the inmost essence of religion, apart from its outward machinery of creed, cult, ceremony and symbol, is the search for God and the finding of God. Its aspiration is to discover the Infinite, the Absolute, the One, the Divine, who is all these things and yet no abstraction but a Being. Its work is a sincere living out of the true and intimate relations between man and God, relations of unity, relations of difference, relations of an illuminated knowledge, an ecstatic love and delight, an absolute surrender and service, a casting of every part of our existence out of its normal status into an uprush of man towards the Divine and a descent of the Divine into man. All this has nothing to do with the realm of reason or its normal activities; its aim, its sphere, its process is suprarational. The knowledge of God is not to be gained by weighing the feeble arguments of reason for or against his existence: it is to be gained only by a self-transcending and absolute consecration, aspiration and experience.

> *Is there no similarity between the mode of religious experience and the method of rational scientific experiment or rational philosophic thinking?*

No. Even in those parts of religious discipline which seem most to resemble scientific experiment, the method is a verification if things which exceed the reason and its timid scope. Even in those parts of religious knowledge which seem most to resemble intellectual operations, the illuminating faculties are not imagination, logic and rational judgment, but revelations, inspirations, intuitions, intuitive discernments that leap down to us from a plane of suprarational light. The love of God is an infinite and absolute feeling which does not admit of any rational limitations and does not use a language of rational worship and adoration; the delight in God is that peace and bliss which passes all understanding. The surrender to God is the surrender of the whole being to a suprarational light, will, power and love, and his service takes no account of the compromises with life which the practical reason of man uses as the best part of its method in the ordinary conduct of mundane existence. Wherever religion really finds itself, wherever it opens itself to its own spirit, — there is plenty of that sort of religious practice which is halting, imperfect, half-sincere, only half-sure of itself and in which reason can get in a word, — its way is absolute and its fruits are ineffable.

Has reason then no part to play in the sphere of religion?

Reason has indeed a part to play in relation to this highest field of our religious being and experience, but that part is quite secondary and subordinate. It cannot lay down the law for the religious life, it cannot determine in its own right the system of divine knowledge; it cannot school and lesson the divine love and delight; it cannot set bounds to spiritual experience or lay its yoke upon the action of the spiritual man.

What then is the true function of reason in relation to religion?

Its sole legitimate sphere is to explain as best it can, in its own language and to the rational and intellectual parts of man, the truths, the experiences, the laws of our suprarational and spiritual existence. That has been the work of spiritual philosophy in the East and — much more crudely and imperfectly done — of theology in the West, a work of great importance at moments like the present when the intellect of mankind after a long wandering is again turning towards the search for the Divine. Here there must inevitably enter a part of those operations proper to the intellect, logical reasoning, inferences from the data given by rational experience, analogies drawn from our knowledge of the apparent facts of existence, appeals even to the physical truths of science, all the apparatus of the intelligent mind in its ordinary workings. But this is the weakest part of spiritual philosophy. It convinces the rational mind only where the intellect is already predisposed to belief, and even if it convinces, it cannot give the true knowledge. Reason is safest when it is content to take the profound truths and experiences of the spiritual being and the spiritual life, just as they are given to it, and throw them into such form, order and language as will make them the most intelligible or the least unintelligible to the reasoning mind. Even then it is not quite safe, for it is apt to harden the order into an intellectual system and to present the form as if it were the essence. And, at best, it has to use a language which is not the very tongue of the suprarational truth but its inadequate translation and, since it is not the ordinary tongue either of the rational intelligence, it is open to non-understanding or misunderstanding by the ordinary reason of mankind. It is well-known to the experience of the spiritual seeker that even the highest philosophising cannot give a true inner knowledge, is not the spiritual light, does not open the gates of experience. All it can do is to address the intellect and, when it has done, to say, "I have tried to give you the truth in a form and system which will make it intelligible and possible to you; if you are intellectually convinced or attracted, you can now seek the real knowledge, but you must seek it by other means which are beyond my province."

But the earlier forms of religion are not always of this pure and sublime type and contain much that is impure, ignorant and crude. Has not reason a better claim for interference in this type of religious life than in the high suprarational type of religious aspiration?

As there is the suprarational life in which religious aspiration finds entirely what it seeks, so too there is also the infrarational life of the instincts, impulses, sensations, crude emotions, vital activities from which all human aspiration takes its beginning. These too feel the touch of the religious sense in man, share its needs and experience, desire its satisfaction. Religion includes this satisfaction also in its scope, and in what is usually called religion it seems even to be the greater part, sometimes to an external view almost the whole; for the supreme purity of spiritual experience does not appear or is glimpsed only through this mixed and turbid current. Much impurity, ignorance, superstition, many doubtful elements must form as the result of this contact and union of our highest tendencies with our lower ignorant nature. Here it would seem that reason has its legitimate part; here surely it can intervene to enlighten, purify, rationalise the play of the instincts and impulses. It would seem that a religious reformation, a movement to substitute a "pure" and rational religion for one that is largely infrarational and impure, would be a distinct advance in the religious development of humanity. To a certain extent this may be, but, owing to the peculiar nature of the religious being, its entire urge towards the suprarational, not without serious qualifications, nor can the rational mind do anything here that is of a high positive value.

Religious forms and systems become effete and corrupt and have to be destroyed, or they lose much of their inner sense and become clouded in knowledge and injurious in practice, and in destroying what is effete or in negating aberrations reason has played an important part in religious history. But in its endeavour to get rid of the superstition and ignorance which have attached themselves to religious forms and symbols, intellectual reason unenlightened by spiritual knowledge tends to deny and, so far as it can, to destroy the truth and the experience which was contained in them. Reformations which give too much to reason and are too negative and protestant, usually create religions which lack in wealth of spirituality and fullness of religious emotion; they are not opulent in their contents; their form and too often their spirit is impoverished, bare and cold. If reason is to play any decisive part, it must be an intuitive rather than an intellectual reason, touched always by spiritual intensity and insight.

Is there then a fundamental discord between the religious spirit and the reason?

The relations of the spirit and the reason need not be, as they too often are in our practice, hostile or without any point of contact. Religion itself need not adopt for its principle the formula "I believe because it is impossible" or Pascal's "I believe because it is absurd". What is impossible or absurd to the unaided reason, becomes real and right to the reason lifted beyond itself by the power of the spirit and irradiated by its light. For then it is dominated by the intuitive mind which is our means of passage to a yet higher principle of knowledge.

The widest spirituality does not exclude or discourage any essential human activity or faculty, but works rather to lift all of them up out of their imperfection and groping ignorance, transforms them by its touch and makes them the instruments of the light, power and joy of the divine being and the divine nature.

VIII

SUPERSTITIONS — POPULAR BELIEFS — OCCULTISM

Most of the religious and other popular beliefs of the ancient times have been discarded as mere superstitions by the scientific-rationalistic mind of modern man. Was there no truth in these beliefs?

The word "superstition" has been habitually used as a convenient club to beat down any belief that does not agree with the ideas of the materialistic reason, that is to say, the physical mind dealing with the apparent law of physical process and seeing no further. It has also been used to dismiss ideas and beliefs not in agreement with one's own idea of what is the rational norm of supraphysical truths as well. For many ages man cherished beliefs that implied a force behind which acted on principles unknown to the physical mind and beyond the witness of the outward reason and the senses. Science came in with a method of knowledge which extended the evidence of this outer field of consciousness, and thought that by this method all existence would become explicable. It swept away at once without examination all the ancient beliefs as so many "superstitions" — true, half-true or false, all went into the dust-bin in one impartial sweep, because they did not rely on the method of physical Science and lay outside its data or were or seemed incompatible with its standpoint. Even in the field of supraphysical experience only so much was admitted as could give a mentally rational explanation of itself according to a certain range of ideas — all the rest, everything that seemed to demand an occult, mystic or below-the-surface origin to explain it, was put aside as so much superstition. Popular beliefs that were the fruit sometimes of imagination but sometimes also of a traditional empirical knowledge or of a right instinct shared naturally the same fate. That all this was a hasty and illegitimate operation, itself based on the "superstition" of the all-sufficiency of the new method which really applies only to a limited field, is now becoming more and more evident. The word superstition is one which should be used either not at all or with great caution. It is evidently an anachronism to apply it to beliefs not accepted by the form of religion one happens oneself to follow or favour.

But surely it can't be denied that there are a number of beliefs which are only blind superstitions.

We cannot go so far as to deny that there is such a thing as superstition — a fixed belief without any ground in something that is quite unsound and does not hang together. But the human mind readily claps on such names to belief in things which can be or are in themselves true, and this is a mixture which very badly confuses the search for knowledge. But precisely because of this mixture, because somewhere behind the superstition or not far off from it there is very usually some real truth, one ought to be cautious in using the word or sweeping away with it as a convenient broom the true, the partly true and the unfounded together and claiming that the bare ground left is the only truth of the matter.

Belief in magical and occult practices was common to all humanity before the advent of modern Science. What is the real nature and function of occultism?

Occultism is in its essence man's effort to arrive at a knowledge of secret truths and potentialities of Nature which will lift him out of slavery to his physical limits of being, an attempt in particular to possess and organise the mysterious, occult, outwardly still undeveloped direct power of Mind upon Life and of both Mind and Life over Matter. There is at the same time an endeavour to establish communication with worlds and entities belonging to the supraphysical heights, depths and intermediate levels of cosmic Being and to utilise this communion for the mastery of a higher Truth and for a help to man in his will to make himself sovereign over Nature's powers and forces.

This human aspiration takes its stand on the belief, intuition or intimation that we are not mere creatures of the mud, but souls, minds, wills that can know all the mysteries of this and every world and become not only Nature's pupils but her adepts and masters. The occultist sought to know the secret of physical things also and in this effort he furthered astronomy, created chemistry, gave an impulse to other sciences, for he utilised geometry also and the science of numbers; but still more he sought to know the secrets of supernature. In this sense occultism might be described as the science of the supernatural; but it is in fact only the discovery of the supraphysical, the surpassing of the material limit, — the heart of occultism is not the impossible chimera which hopes to go beyond or outside all force of Nature and make pure phantasy and arbitrary miracle omnipotently effective. What seems to us supernatural is in fact either a spontaneous irruption of the phenomena of other-Nature into physical Nature or, in the work of the occultist, a possession of the knowledge and power of the higher orders or grades of cosmic Being and Energy and the direction of their forces and processes towards the production of effects in the physical world by seizing on possibilities of interconnection and means for a material effectuality. There are powers of the mind and the life-force which have not been included in Nature's present systematisation of mind and life in matter, but are potential and can be brought to bear upon material things and happenings or even brought in and added to the present systematisation so as to enlarge the control of mind over our own life and body or to act on the minds, lives, bodies of others or on the movements of cosmic Forces. The modern admission of hypnotism is an example of such a discovery and systematised application, — though still narrow and limited, limited by its method and formula, — of occult powers which otherwise touch us only by a casual or a hidden action whose process is unknown to us or imperfectly caught by a few; for we are all the time undergoing a battery of suggestions, thought-suggestions, impulse-suggestions, will-suggestions, emotional and sensational suggestions, thought-waves, life-waves that come on us or into us from others or from the universal Energy, but act and produce their effects without our knowledge. A systematised endeavour to know these movements and their law and possibilities, to master and use the power or nature-force behind them or to protect ourselves from them would fall within one province of occultism: but it would only be a small part even of that province; for wide and multiple are the possible fields, uses, processes of this vast range of little-explored Knowledge.

What was the essential difference between occultism as practised in the West and in the East?

Occultism in the West indulged too freely in the romance of the supernatural or made the mistake of concentrating its major effort on the discovery of formulas and effective modes for using supernormal powers. It deviated into magic, white and black or into a romantic or thaumaturgic paraphernalia of occult mysticism and the exaggeration of what was after all a limited and scanty knowledge. These tendencies and this insecurity of mental foundation made it difficult to defend and easy to discredit, a target facile and vulnerable. In Egypt and the East this line of knowledge arrived at a greater and more comprehensive endeavour: this ampler maturity can be seen still intact in the remarkable system of the Tantras; it was not only a many-sided science of the supernormal but supplied the basis of all the occult elements of religion and even developed a great and powerful system of spiritual discipline and self-realisation.

In the popular mind occultism is usually associated with magic and magical formulas like the mantras. The rationalist mind considers these as fraudulent tricks intended to deceive credulous people. Is there no effective truth in these formulas?

This is only one side of occultism but it is not altogether a superstition as is vainly imagined by those who have not looked deeply or at all at this covert side of secret Nature-Force or experimented with its possibilities. Formulas and their application, a mechanisation of latent forces, can be astonishingly effective in the occult use of mind-power and life-power just as it is in physical Science, but this is only a subordinate method and a limited direction.

What should be the highest and most important aim of the occult or magical practice?

Its most important aim must be the discovery of the hidden truths and powers of the mind-force and the life-power and the greater forces of the concealed spirit. The highest occultism is that which discovers the secret movements and dynamic supernormal possibilities of Mind and Life and Spirit and uses them in their native force or by an applied process for the greater effectivity of our mental, vital and spiritual being.

IX

COMMUNICATIONS WITH THE DEAD — SUPERNATURAL PHENOMENA

A section of scientists in Europe who could not deny the occurrence of supernatural phenomena have tried in recent times to investigate them by scientific experimentation and collected a mass of evidence in this field, especially in the psychical research societies organised for the purpose. Communications with the dead through spiritual seances has been a subject of special interest in these societies. Is there any truth in the claim made by them that it is possible to have communication with dead persons through a "psychic" medium?

There is after death a period in which one passes through the other worlds and it is quite possible for the dead or rather the departed — for they are not dead — who are still in regions near the earth to have communication with the living; sometimes it happens automatically, sometimes by an effort at communication on one side of the curtain or the other. There is no impossibility of such communication by the means used by the spiritists.

But are not a large number of communications received by mediums in the seances quite false?

Usually, genuine communications or contacts of that kind or brought about by that means can only be with those who are yet in a world which is a sort of idealised replica of the earth-consciousness and in which the same personality, ideas, memories persist that the person had here. But all that pretends to be such communications with departed souls is not genuine, especially when it is done through a paid professional medium.

Why do these mediums receive false communications?

It is because there is an enormous amount of mixture of a very undesirable kind — for apart from the great mass of unconscious suggestions from the sitters or the contributions of the medium's subliminal consciousness, one gets into contact with a world of beings which is of a very deceptive or self-deceptive illusory nature. Many of these come and claim to be the departed souls of relatives, acquaintances, well-known men, famous personalities, etc. There are also beings who pick up the discarded feelings and memories of the dead and masquerade with them. There are a great number of beings who come to such seances only to play with the consciousness of men or exercise their powers through this contact with the earth and who dope the mediums and sitters with their falsehoods, tricks and illusions. (This refers, of course, to the mediums who are not themselves tricksters.) What comes through the medium may be thus a mixture of the medium's subconscient (using subconscient in the ordinary, not in the Yogic sense) and that of the sitters; there may be an intervention from something like conscious vital sheaths left by the departed or perhaps occupied or used by some spirit or some vital being. The departed himself in his vital sheath or in something else assumed for the occasion may intervene; the communication in either case is from his vital part. Or some elemental spirit of the lowest vital-physical world near earth may interfere. Where there is such a mixture, a horrible confusion can for the most part be the result — a hotch-potch of all sorts of things coming in through the medium of an atmosphere of "astral" grey light and shadow.

Sometimes these mediums claim to contact the departed souls of the great men of the past like Christ, Buddha, Shakespeare, Napoleon, etc., and to receive communications from them. Are these communications genuine?

All such pretended communications with the famous dead of long-past times are in their very nature deceptive and most of those with the recent ones also — that is evident from the character of these communications.

Is the possibility of genuine communication with dead persons then very rare?

Through conscientious mediums one may get sound results, but even these are very ignorant of the nature of the forces they are handling and have no discrimination which can guard them against trickery from the other side of the veil.

Does this mean that there is little hope of getting true knowledge of the after-life through the spiritualistic seances?

Very little genuine knowledge of the nature of the after-life can be gathered from these seances; a true knowledge is more often gained by the experience of individuals who make serious contact or are able in one way or another to cross the border.

Is it quite safe to take part in these seances and psychical societies?

Such seances can put one in *rapport* with a very low world of vital beings and forces, themselves obscure, incoherent or tricky and it is dangerous to associate with such a world or to undergo any influence. A contact with such a level of beings can be harmful and spiritually dangerous. Many mediums become nervously or morally unbalanced.

It is said that it is the "ghost" of the dead person who comes to these seances. The term "ghost" is also often used in other connections, e.g. in the case of haunted houses. Belief in ghosts, in fact, was universal till the advent of modern science. Is there any truth in this belief?

The word "ghost" as used in popular parlance covers an enormous number of distinct phenomena which have no necessary connection with each other. To name a few only:
 (1) An actual contact with the soul of a human being in its

subtle body and transcribed to our mind by the appearance of an image or the hearing of a voice.

(2) A mental formation stamped by the thoughts and feelings of a departed human being on the atmosphere of a place or locality, wandering about there or repeating itself, till that formation either exhausts itself or is dissolved by one means or another. This is the explanation of such phenomena as the haunted house in which the scenes attending or surrounding or preceding a murder are repeated over and over again and many other similar phenomena.

(3) A being of the lower vital planes who has assumed the discarded vital sheath of a departed human being or a fragment of his vital personality and appears and acts in the form and perhaps with the surface thoughts and memories of that person.

(4) A being of the lower vital plane who by the medium of a living human being or by some other means or agency is able to materialise itself sufficiently so as to appear and act in a visible form or speak with an audible voice or, without so appearing, to move about material things, e.g., furniture or to materialise objects or to shift them from place to place. This accounts for what are called *poltergeists*, phenomena of stone-throwing, tree-inhabiting *bhūtas*, and other well-known phenomena.

(5) Apparitions which are the formations of one's own mind and take to the senses an objective appearance.

(6) Temporary possession of people by vital beings who sometimes pretend to be departed relatives, etc.

(7) Thought-images of themselves projected, often by people at the moment of death, which appear at that time or a few hours afterwards to their friends or relatives.

Is there any truth in what are called the "automatic writings" recorded by the "spiritualists"?

Automatic writings like communications with the dead are a mixed affair. Part comes from the subconscious mind of the medium and part from that of the sitters. But it is not true that all can be accounted for by a dramatising imagination and memory. Sometimes there are things none present could know or remember; sometimes even, though that is rare, glimpses of the future.

> *What is the explanation of such phenomena as dematerialisation, rematerialisation, levitation, etc. known to many Yogis in India and Tibetan Lamas? Are they merely tricks or magic as is usually supposed?*

There are different planes of substance, gross, subtle and more subtle going back to what is called causal (*kāraṇa*) substance. What is more gross can be reduced to the subtle state and the subtle brought into the gross state; that accounts for dematerialisation and rematerialisation. These are occult processes and are vulgarly regarded as magic. Ordinarily the magician knows nothing of the why and wherefore of what he is doing, he has simply learned the formula or process or else controls elemental beings of the subtler states (planes or worlds) who do the thing for him. The Tibetans indulge widely in occult processes; the books of Madame David Neel who has lived in Tibet give an idea of their expertness in these things. But also the Tibetan Lamas know something of the laws of occult (mental and vital) energy and how it can be made to act on physical things. That is something which goes beyond mere magic. The direct power of mind-force or life-force upon Matter can be extended to an almost illimitable degree. It must be remembered that Energy is fundamentally one in all the planes, only taking more and more dense forms, so there is nothing *a priori* impossible in mind-energy or life-energy acting directly on material energy and substance; if they do, they can make a material object do things or rather can do things with a material object which would be to that object in its ordinary poise or "law" unhabitual and therefore apparently impossible.

X

THE PROBLEM OF GOOD AND EVIL (1)

One of the most persistent problems of mankind throughout the ages has been the problem of good and evil or the ethical problem. It has been viewed in different ways at different times. Some ancient religions tried to fix an absolute code of conduct based upon supreme laws of good and evil revealed by God through a prophet and having authority at all times and at all places. The Ten Commandments of the ancient Hebrews are an example of this tendency. Is there any truth in the divine origin of these codes and do they possess the eternal validity ascribed to them? What is the difference between the nature of the true divine law and these inflexible codes?

These codes are for the most part no more than idealistic glorifications of the moral principles sanctified by religious emotion with the label of a superhuman origin. Some, like the extreme Christian ethic, are rejected by human nature because they insist unworkably on an impracticable absolute rule. Others prove in the end to be evolutionary compromises and become obsolete in the march of Time. The true divine law, unlike these mental counterfeits, cannot be a system of rigid ethical determinations that press into their cast-iron moulds all our life-movements. The Law divine is truth of life and truth of the spirit and must take up with a free living plasticity and inspire with the direct touch of its eternal light each step of our action and all the complexities of our life-issues. It must act not as a rule and formula but as an enveloping and penetrating conscious presence that determines all our thoughts, activities, feelings, impulses of will by its infallible power and knowledge.

Some other older religions erected complex Shastras like the codes of Manu and Confucius and proclaimed them as the expression of everlasting verities, Sanatan Dharma. Is

> *the claim of these Shastras to be the expression of supreme and eternal truths of conduct valid? Do they serve the highest ethical aspiration of our nature?*

The Shastra is a combination of some kind of uniting amalgam of three principles — the social rule, the moral law and certain principles of our highest nature. The first two principles are evolutionary and valid for a time, mental constructions, human readings of the will of the Eternal; the third, attached and subdued to certain social and moral formulas, had to share the fortunes of its forms. Either the Shastras grows obsolete and has to be progressively changed or finally cast away or else it stands as a rigid barrier to the self-development of the individual and the race. The Shastra erects a collective and external standard; it ignores the inner nature of the individual, the indeterminable elements of a secret spiritual force within him. But the nature of the individual will not be ignored; its demand is inexorable. The unrestrained indulgence of his outer impulses leads to anarchy and dissolution, but the suppression and coercion of his soul's freedom by a fixed and mechanical rule spells stagnation or an inner death. Not his coercion or determination from outside, but the free discovery of his highest spirit and the truth of an eternal movement is the supreme thing that he has to effectuate.

> *The ethical idealist looks for the sure criterion of his conduct not in any superhuman or divine agency but in his own moral reason. Kant, for example, maintains that the moral law is inherent in human reason itself; it is* a priori, *before experience, innate in the very nature of the human mind, a categorical imperative, an unfailing determinant of right and wrong. Has human reason this inherent and categorical moral sense?*

The rational ethical idealist has tried to reduce the ethical life like all the rest to a matter of reason, to determine its nature, its law, its practical action by some principle of reason, by some law of reason. He has never really succeeded and he never can really succeed; his appearances of success are mere pretences of the intellect building elegant and empty constructions with words and ideas, mere conventions of logic and vamped-up syntheses, in sum, pretentious failures which break down at the first strenuous touch of reality. Our moral ideals are themselves for the most part ill-evolved, ignorant and arbitrary, mental constructions rather than transcriptions of the eternal truths of the spirit. Authoritative and dogmatic, they assert certain absolute standards in theory, but in practice every existing system of ethics proves either in application unworkable or is in fact a constant coming short of the absolute standard to which the ideal pretends. Moreover, these absolute standards themselves become conflicting principles in their present application by an imperfect humanity. Justice often demands what love abhors. Right reason dispassionately considering the facts of nature and human relations in search of a satisfying norm or rule is unable to admit without modification either any reign of absolute justice or any reign of absolute love. And in fact man's absolute justice easily turns out to be in practice a sovereign injustice; for his mind, one-sided and rigid in its constructions, puts forward a one-sided partial and rigorous scheme or figure and claims for it totality and absoluteness and an application that ignores the subtler truth of things and the plasticity of life. All our standards turned into action either waver on a flux of compromises or err by this partiality and unelastic structure.

But is it not a fact that, in spite of its basic limitations, the ethical idealist's cult of absolute moral standards and categorical imperatives of an ideal moral law has been a great force for the moral improvement and growth of humanity?

There is, no doubt, something here that helps us to rise beyond limitation by the physical and vital man in us, an insistence that overpasses the individual and collective needs and desires of a humanity still bound to the living mud of Matter in which it took its roots, an aspiration that helps to develop the mental and moral being in us: this new sublimating element has been therefore an acquisition of great importance; its workings have marked a considerable step forward in the difficult evolution of terrestrial Nature. And behind the inadequacy of these ethical conceptions something too is concealed that does attach to a supreme Truth; there is here the glimmer of a light and power that are part of a yet unreached divine Nature. But the mental idea of these things is not that light and the moral formulation of them is not that power. These are only representative constructions of the mind that cannot embody the divine spirit which they vainly endeavour to imprison in their categorical formulas. Our inner nature is the progressive expression of the eternal Spirit and too complex a power to be tied by a single dominant mental or moral principle. Beyond the mental and moral being in us is a greater divine being that is spiritual and supramental. Only the supramental consciousness can reveal to the differing and conflicting forces of our nature their spiritual truth and harmonise their divergences.

Recent thinkers have treated the ethical problem more as a practical question of social relationship rather than that of ideal or divine absolute laws. Thus the utilitarian school of the nineteenth century, of which Mill was one of the chief representatives, laid down the dictum of "the greatest good of the greatest number" as the sole criterion of all ethical conduct. Can this principle of utility be considered the true standard of ethical good and evil?

Utility is a fundamental principle of existence and all fundamental principles of existence are in the end one; therefore it is true that the highest good is also the highest utility. It is true also that, not any balance of the greatest good of the greatest number, but simply the good of others and most widely the good of all is the one ideal aim of our outgoing ethical practice; it is that which the ethical man would like to effect, if he could only find the way and be always sure what is the real good of all. But this does not help to regulate our ethical practice, nor does it supply us with its inner principle whether of being or of action, but only produces one of the many considerations by which we can feel our way along the road which is so difficult to travel. Good, not utility, must be the principle and standard of good; otherwise we fall into the hands of that dangerous pretender expediency, whose whole method is alien to the ethical. Moreover, the standard of utility, the judgment of utility, its spirit, its form, its application must vary with the individual nature, the habit of mind, the outlook on the world. Here there can be no reliable general law to which all can subscribe, no set of large governing principles such as it is sought to supply to our conduct by a true ethics. Nor can ethics at all or ever be a matter of calculation. There is only one safe rule for the ethical man, to stick to his principle of good, his instinct for good, his vision of good, his intuition of good and to govern by that his conduct. He may err, but he will be on his right road in spite of all stumblings, because he will be faithful to the law of his nature. The saying of the Gita is always true: better is the law of one's own nature though ill-performed, dangerous is an alien law however speciously superior it may seem to our reason. But the law of nature of the ethical being is the pursuit of good; it can never be the pursuit of utility.

XI

THE PROBLEM OF GOOD AND EVIL (2)

The hedonistic theory of ethics judges virtue from the standard of pleasure or satisfaction which it considers to be the goal of all human activity and man's supreme good. How far can this be admitted as the true aim of our ethical endeavour?

Neither the pursuit of pleasure high or base nor self-satisfaction of any kind, however subtle or even spiritual, can be the law of nature of the ethical being. It is true that the highest good is both in its nature and inner effect the highest bliss. Ananda, delight of being, is the spring of all existence and that to which it tends and for which it seeks openly or covertly in all its activities. It is true too that in virtue growing, in good accomplished there is a great pleasure and that the seeking for it may well be always there as a subconscient motive to the pursuit of virtue. But for practical purposes this is a side aspect of the matter; it does not constitute pleasure into a test or standard of virtue. On the contrary, virtue comes to the natural man by a struggle with his pleasure-seeking nature and is often a deliberate embracing of pain, an edification of strength by suffering. We do not embrace that pain and struggle for the pleasure of the pain and the pleasure of the struggle; for that higher strenuous delight, though it is felt by the secret spirit in us, is not usually or not at first conscious in the conscient normal part of our being which is the field of the struggle. The action of the ethical man is not motived by even an inner pleasure, but by a call of his being, necessity of an ideal, the figure of an absolute standard, a law of the Divine.

But the history of the human race shows that the origin of man's morality and the determining cause of its evolution is not his inner necessity for an ideal but the social need of adjusting his personal claims and desires to those of the others in society. Is not this social need the true origin of morality?

It is true that this social need is the obscure matrix of morality and of man's ethical impulse and that, in the outward history, the evolution of man in society may seem to be the determining cause of his ethical evolution. For ethics only begins by the demand upon him of something other than his personal preference, vital pleasure or material self-interest; and this demand seems at first to work on him through the necessity of his relations with others, by the exigencies of his social existence. But that this is not the core of the matter is shown by the fact that the ethical demand does not always square with the social demand, nor the ethical standard always coincide with the social standard. On the contrary, the ethical man is often called upon to reject and do battle with the social demand, to break, to move away from, to reverse the social standard. His relations with others and his relations with himself are both of them the occasions of his ethical growth; but that which determines his ethical being is his relations with God, the urge of the Divine upon him whether concealed in his nature or conscious in his higher self or inner genius. He obeys an inner ideal, not an outer standard; he answers to a divine law in his being, not to a social claim or a collective necessity. The ethical imperative comes not from around, but from within him and above him.

What are the progressive stages of the growth of man's moral nature?

Our ethical impulses and activities begin like all the rest in the infrarational and take their rise from the subconscient. They arise as an instinct of right, an instinct of obedience to an ununder-stood law, an instinct of self-giving in labour, an instinct of sacrifice and self-sacrifice, an instinct of love, of self-subordination and of solidarity with others. Man obeys the law at first without any inquiry into the why and the wherefore; he does not seek for it a sanction in the reason. His first thought is that it is a law created by higher powers than himself and his race and he says with the ancient poet that he knows not whence these laws sprang, but only that they are and endure and cannot with impunity be violated. What the instincts and impulses seek after, the reason labours to make us understand, so that the will may come to use the ethical impulses intelligently and turn the instincts into ethical ideas. It corrects man's crude and often erring misprisions of the ethical instinct, separates and purifies his confused associations, shows as best it can the relations of his often clashing moral ideals, tries to arbitrate and compromise between their conflicting claims, arranges a system and many-sided rule of ethical action. And all this is well, a necessary stage of our advance, but in the end these ethical ideas and this intelligent ethical will which it has tried to train to its control, escape from its hold and soar up beyond its province. Always, even when enduring its rein and curb, they have that inborn tendency.

Why does the developing ethical impulse in man finally refuse to follow the dictates of his reason?

The ethical being of man like the rest is a growth and a seeking towards the absolute, the divine, which can only be attained securely in the suprarational. It seeks after an absolute purity, an absolute right, an absolute truth, an absolute strength, an absolute love and self-giving, and it is most satisfied when it can get them in absolute measure, without limit, curb or compromise, divinely, infinitely, in a sort of godhead and transfiguration of the ethical being. The reason is chiefly concerned with what it best understands, the apparent process, the machinery, the outward act, its result and effect, its circumstance, occasion and motive; by these it judges the morality of the action and the morality of the doer. But the developed ethical being knows instinctively that it is an inner something which it seeks and the outward act is only a means of bringing out and manifesting within ourselves by its psychological effects that inner absolute and eternal entity.

The Problem of Good and Evil (2)   51

By what standard does the developed ethical man measure the value of his actions?

To the developed ethical being the value of our actions is not so much in their apparent nature and outward results as in their help towards the growth of the Divine within us. It is difficult, even impossible to justify upon outward grounds the absolute justice, absolute right, absolute purity, love or selflessness of an action or course of action; for action is always relative, it is mixed and uncertain in its results, perplexed in its occasions. But it is possible to relate the inner being to the eternal and absolute good, to make our sense and will full of it so as to act out of its impulsion or its intuitions and inspirations. That is what the ethical being labours towards and the higher ethical man increasingly attains to in his inner efforts.

What is the true essence of ethics and how is it realised?

Ethics is not in its essence a calculation of good and evil in the action or a laboured effort to be blameless according to the standards of the world, — those are only crude appearances, — it is an attempt to grow into the divine nature. Its parts of purity are an aspiration towards the inalienable purity of God's being; its parts of truth and right are a seeking after conscious unity with the law of the divine knowledge and will; its parts of sympathy and charity are a movement towards the infinity and universality of the divine love; its parts of strength and manhood are an edification of the divine strength and power. That is the heart of its meaning. Its high fulfilment comes when the being of the man undergoes this transfiguration; when it is not his actions that standardise his nature but his nature that gives value to his actions; then he is no longer laboriously virtuous, artificially moral, but naturally divine. Actively, too, he is fulfilled and consummated when he is not led or moved either by the infrarational impulses or the rational intelligence and will, but inspired and piloted by the divine knowledge and will made conscious in his nature. And that can only be done, first by communication of the truth of these things through the intuitive mind as it purifies itself progressively from the invasion of egoism, self-interest, desire, passion and all kinds of self-will, finally through the suprarational light and power, no longer communicated but present and in possession of his being. Such was the supreme aim of the ancient sages who had the wisdom which rational man and rational society have rejected because it was too high a truth for the comprehension of the reason and for the powers of the normal limited human will too bold and immense, too infinite an effort.

XII

THE PROBLEM OF GOOD AND EVIL (3)

The moralist enjoins the practice of virtue by laying down the dictum that good must create good and evil must create evil in accordance with the law that like creates like. "Do unto others as you would be done by," he says, because then they will indeed so do to you. The strict pacifist, for example, would never admit the use of violence or a resort to war in any circumstances whatsoever on the ground that violence leads always to further violence. Does any such strict rule of moral return prevail in actual life?

The rule is true to a certain extent in tendency and works sometimes well enough and the prudential intelligence of man takes some account of it in action, but it is not true all the way and all the time. It is evident enough that hatred, violence, injustice are likely to create an answering hatred, violence and injustice and that I can only indulge these propensities with impunity if I am sufficiently powerful to defy resistance or so long as I am at once strong and prudent enough to provide against their natural reactions. It is true also that by doing good and kindness I create a certain good-will in others and can rely under ordinary or favourable circumstances not so much on gratitude and return in kind as on their support and favour. But this good and this evil are both of them movements of the ego, and on the mixed egoism of human nature there can be no safe or positive reliance. An egoistic selfish strength, if it knows what to do and where to stop, even a certain measure of violence and injustice, if it is strong and skilful, cunning, fraud, many kinds of evil, do actually pay in man's dealing with man hardly less than in the animal's with the animal, and on the other hand the doer of good who counts on a return or reward finds himself as often as not disappointed of his bargained recompense.

Why is this so?

It is because the weakness of human nature worships the power that tramples on it, does homage to successful strength, can return to every kind of strong or skilful imposition, belief, acceptance, obedience: it can crouch and fawn and admire even amidst movements of hatred and terror; it has singular loyalties and unreasoning instincts. And its disloyalties too are as unreasoning or light and fickle: it takes just dealing and beneficence as its right and forgets or cares not to repay. And there is worse; for justice, mercy, beneficence, kindness are often enough rewarded by their opposites and ill-will an answer to good-will is a brutally common experience. If something in the world and in man returns good for good and evil for evil, it as often returns evil for good and, with or without a conscious moral intention, good for evil. And even an unegoistic virtue or a divine good and love entering the world awakens hostile reactions. Attila and Jenghiz on the throne to the end, Christ on the cross and Socrates drinking his portion of hemlock are no very clear evidence for any optimistic notion of a law of moral return in the world of human nature.

If not in human nature, does this law operate in the action of the larger world measures?

There is little more sign of its sure existence in the world measures. Actually in the cosmic dispensation evil comes out of good and good out of evil and there seems to be no exact correspondence between the moral and the vital measures. All that we can say is that good done tends to increase the sum and total power of good in the world and the greater this grows, the greater is likely to be the sum of human happiness, and that evil done tends to increase the sum and total power of evil in the world and the greater this grows, the greater is likely to be the sum of human suffering and, eventually, man or nation doing evil has in some way to pay for it, but not often in any intelligibly graded or apportioned measure and not always in clearly translating terms of vital good fortune and ill-fortune.

The Problem of Good and Evil (3)

Does this rule of moral return correspond to the true principle and the whole law of ethics?

It cannot, because good and evil are moral and not vital values and have a clear right only to a moral and not a vital return, because reward and punishment put forward as the conditions of good-doing and evil-doing do not constitute and cannot create a really moral order, the principle itself, whatever temporary end it serves, being fundamentally immoral from the higher point of view of a true and pure ethics, and because there are other forces that count and have their right — knowledge, power and many others. The correspondence of moral and vital good is a demand of the human ego and like many others of its demands answers to certain tendencies in the world mind, but is not its whole law or highest purpose. A moral order there can be, but it is in ourselves and for its own sake that we have to create it and, only when we have so created it and found its right relation to other powers of life, can we hope to make it count as its full value in the right ordering of man's vital existence.

Is there not a retaliatory action in Nature, a sort of a boomerang movement of energy by which the results of a man's actions rebound upon him, sometimes in exact figure and measure? The ancients recognised this action of Nature and called it the law of talion which seemed to them a sufficient evidence of a moral order in the universe. Does any such law of exact and unfailing retributive rebound exist in Nature?

The careful thinker will pause long before he hastens to subscribe to any such conclusion, for there is much that militates against it and this kind of definite reaction is rather exceptional than an ordinary rule of human life. If it were a regular feature, men would soon learn the code of the draconic impersonal legislator and know what to avoid and the list of life's prohibitions and vetoes. But there is no such clear penal legislation of Nature.

The mathematical precision of physical Nature's action and reaction cannot indeed be expected from mental and vital Nature. For not only does everything become infinitely more subtle, complex and variable as we rise in the scale, so that in our life-action there is an extraordinary intertwining of forces and mixture of many values, but, even, the psychological and moral value of the same action differs in different cases, according to the circumstance, the conditions, the motive and mind of the doer.

But in the dealings of man with man and of man with the universe and God, would not this law work out a strict ethical justice?

The law of the talion is no just or ethical rule when applied by man to men and, applied by a superhuman dispenser of justice or impersonal law with a crude rule of thumb to the delicate and intricate tangle of man's life-action and life-motives, it would be no better. And it is evident too that the slow, long and subtle purposes of the universal Power working in the human race would be defeated rather than served by any universality of this too precise and summary procedure. Accordingly we find that its working is occasional and intermittent rather than regular, variable and to our minds capricious rather than automatic and plainly intelligible.

But how is it then that in a number of cases a definite and unmistakable recoil of a man's actions comes upon him sooner or later?

At times in the individual's life the rebound of this kind of Karma is decisively, often terribly clear and penal justice is done, although it may come to him in an unexpected fashion, long delayed and from strange quarters; but however satisfactory to our dramatic sense, this is not the common method of retributive Nature. Her ways are more tortuous, subtle, unobtrusive and indecipherable. Sometimes a nation pays for its crimes or offences though not with that kind of precision but still enough for the sign manual of the law to be there, but individually it is the innocent who suffer.

Is there no truth then in man's idea of this law of talion? Does it not serve any moral purpose in the will and the workings of the universe?

It is evident that we cannot make much of a force that works out in so strange a fashion, however occasionally striking and dramatic its pointing at cause and consequence. It is too uncertain in its infliction of penalty to serve the end which the human mind expects from a system of penal justice, too inscrutably variable in its incidence to act as an indicator to that element in the human temperament which waits upon expediency and regulates its steps by a prudential eye to consequence. Men and nations continue to act always in the same fashion regardless of this occasional breaking out of the lightnings of a retaliatory doom, these occasional precisions of Karmic justice amidst the uncertainties of the complex measures of the universe. It works really not on the mind and will of man — except to some degree in a subtle and imperfect fashion on the subconscient mind — but outside him, as a partial check and regulator helping to maintain the balance of the returns of energy and the life purposes of the world-spirit. The action of Nature's penalties, seldom agreeing with any pure law of the talion, is intended to prevent the success of the vital egoism of man and serves as an interim compression and compulsion until he can discover and succeed in spite of his vital self in obeying a higher law of his being and a purer dynamism of motive in his directing mind and governing spirit. It serves therefore a certain moral purpose in the will in the universe, but is not itself, even in combination with others, sufficient to be the law of a moral order.

XIII

THE LAW OF KARMA

Belief in the law of Karma, in one form or other, has existed both in the East and the West since ancient times. Is this belief based on any sound practical or philosophical truth?

There is an unanswerable truth in the theory of Karma, — not necessarily in the form the ancients gave to it, but in the idea at its centre, — which at once strikes the mind and commands the assent of the understanding. There is a solidity at once of philosophic and of practical truth supporting the idea, a bed-rock of the deepest universal undeniable verities against which the human mind must always come up in its fathomings of the fathomless; in this way indeed does the world deal with us, there is a law here which does so make itself felt and against which all our egoistic ignorance and self-will and violence dashes up in the end, as the old Greek poet said of the haughty insolence and prosperous pride of man, against the very foundation of the throne of Zeus, the marble feet of Themis, the adamantine bust of Ananke. There is the secret of an eternal factor, the base of the unchanging action of the just and truthful gods, *devaanaam dhruva vrataani*, in the self-sufficient and impartial law of Karma.

What is the fundamental meaning of Karma?

Fundamentally, the meaning of Karma is that all existence is the working of a universal Energy, a process and an action and a building of things by that action, — an unbuilding too, but as a step to further building, — that all is a continuous chain in which every one link is bound indissolubly to the past infinity of numberless links, and the whole governed by fixed relations, by a fixed association of cause and effect, present action the result of past action as future action will be the result of present action, all cause a working of energy and all effect too a working of energy. The moral significance is that all our existence is a putting out of an energy which is in us and by which we are made and as is the nature of the energy which is put forth as cause, so shall be that of the energy which returns as effect, that this is the universal law and nothing in the world can, being of and in our world, escape from its governing incidence.That is the philosophical reality of the theory of Karma, and that too is the way of seeing which has been developed by physical Science.

It is held by many that this law of Karma wholly determines and governs the evolution of the life and the soul in the universe. Is this true?

The law or chain of Karma is only an outward machinery and cannot be elevated to a greater position as the sole and absolute determinant of the life-workings of the cosmos, unless the cosmos is itself entirely mechanical in its character. But all is not Law and Process, there is also Being and Consciousness; there is not only a machinery but a Spirit in things, not only Nature and law of cosmos but a cosmic Spirit, not only a process of mind and life and body but a soul in the natural creature. If it were not so, there could be no rebirth of a soul and no field for a law of Karma. But if the fundamental truth of our being is spiritual and not mechanical, it must be our self, our soul that fundamentally determines its own evolution, and the law of Karma can only be one of the processes it uses for that purpose: our Spirit, our Self must be greater than its Karma. There is Law, but there is also spiritual freedom. Law and process are one side of our existence and their reign is over our outer mind, life and body, for these are mostly subject to the mechanism of Nature. But even here their mechanical power is absolute only over body and Matter; for Law becomes more complex and less rigid, Process more plastic and less mechanical when there comes in the phenomenon of Life, and yet more is this so when Mind intervenes with its subtlety; an inner freedom already begins to intervene and, the more we go within, the soul's power of choice is increasingly felt: for Prakriti is the field of law and process, but the soul, the Purusha, is the giver of the sanction, *anumantā,* and even if ordinarily it chooses to remain a witness and concede an automatic sanction, it can be, if it wills, the master of its nature, Ishwara.

The modern scientific mind, while admitting the mechanical law of the action of the energies, reduces all to a determination by the physical energies of the universe. Is this not an arbitrary over-simplification of the complex workings of the many strands of the universal Nature? Is not the action of our inner mental and moral nature largely independent of the rule of our bodily processes?

Being is no doubt one, and Law too may be one; but it is perilous to fix from the beginning on one type of phenomena with a predetermined will to deduce from that all other phenomena however different in its significance and nature. In that way we are bound to distort truth into the mould of our own prepossession. Intermediately at least we have rather to recognise the old harmonious truths of Veda, — which also came by this way in its end, its Vedanta, to the conception of the unity of Being, — that there are different planes of cosmic existence and therefore too of our own existence and in each of them the same powers, energies or laws must act in a different type and in another sense and light of their effectuality. First, then, we see that if Karma be a universal truth or the universal truth of being, it must be equally true of the inly-born mental and moral worlds of our action as in our outward relations with the physical universe. It is the mental energy that we put forth which determines the mental effect, — but subject to all the impact of past, present and future surrounding circumstance, because we are not isolated powers in the world, but rather our energy is a subordinate strain and thread of the universal energy. The moral energy of our action determines similarly the nature and effect of the moral consequence, but subject too, — though to this element the rigid moralist does not give sufficient consideration, — to the same incidence of past, present and future surrounding circumstance. That this is true of the output of physical energy needs no saying nor any demonstration. We must recognise these different types and variously formulated motions of the one universal Force, and it will not do to say from the beginning that the measure and quality of my inner being is some result of the output of a physical energy translated into mental and moral energies, — for instance, that my doing a good or a bad action or yielding to good or to bad affections and motives is at the mercy of my liver, or contained in the physical germ of my birth, or is the effect of my chemical elements or determined essentially and ultimately by the disposition of the constituent electrons of my brain and nervous system. Whatever drafts my mental and moral being may make on the corporeal for its supporting physical energy and however it may be affected by its borrowings, yet it is very evident that it uses them for other and larger purposes, has a supraphysical method, evolves much greater motives and significances. The moral energy is in itself a distinct power, has its own plane of Karma, moves me even, and that characteristically, to override my vital and physical nature. Forms of one universal Force at bottom — or at top — these may be, but in practice they are different energies and have to be so dealt with — until we can find what that universal Force may be in its highest purest texture and initial power and whether that discovery can give us in the perplexities of our nature a unifying direction.

The ethical mind has tried to read in the complex workings of the Karmic Law the strict working of the rule of moral justice. Is this also not an error of over-simplification by arbitrary selection of a limited principle as the sole regulator of the manifold action of the universal Nature?

The universe is not solely an ethical proposition, a problem of the antinomy of the good and the evil; the Spirit of the universe can in no way be imagined as a rigid moralist concerned only with making all things obey the law of moral good, or a stream of tendency towards righteousness attempting, hitherto with only a very poor success, to prevail and rule, or a stern Justicer rewarding and punishing creatures in a world that he has made or has suffered to be full of wickedness and suffering and evil. The universal Will has evidently many other and more supple modes than that, an infinity of interests, many other elements of its being to manifest, many lines to follow, many laws and purposes to pursue. The law of the world is not this alone that our good brings good to us and our evil brings evil, nor is its key the ethical-hedonistic rule that our moral good brings to us happiness and success and our moral evil brings to us sorrow and misfortune. There is a rule of right in the world, but it is the right of the truth of Nature and of the truth of the Spirit, and that is a vast and various rule and takes many forms that have to be understood and accepted before we can reach either its highest or its integral principle.

Some extreme moralists maintain that even catastrophes and upheavals in the physical nature like earthquakes are a result of the sins of men. Is there any truth in this?

Why should earthquakes occur by some wrong movement of man? When man was not there, did not earthquakes occur? If he were blotted out by poison gas or otherwise, would they cease? Earthquakes are a perturbation in Nature due to some pressure of forces; frequency of earthquakes may coincide with a violence of upheavals in human life but the upheavals of earth and human life are both results of a general clash or pressure of forces, one is not the cause of the other.

XIV

KARMA AND FREE-WILL

If the law of Karma governs everything there can be no possibility of freedom. Are we completely bound by the rule of Karma? Is the human idea of freedom only an illusion?

The world of Matter seems to know nothing about freedom; everything there appears as if written in sibyllic laws upon tablets of stone, laws which have a process, but no initial reason, serve a harmony of purposes or at least produce a cosmos of fixed results, but do not appear to be shaped with an eye to them by any discoverable Intelligence. We can think of no presence of soul in natural things, because we can see in them no conscious action of mind, and a conscious active mental intelligence is to our notions the very basis and standing-ground, if not the whole stuff of soul-existence. If Matter is all, then we may very easily conclude that all is a Karma of material energy which is governed by some inherent incomprehensible mechanically legislating Necessity. But then we see that Life seems to be made of a different stuff; here various possibility develops, here creation becomes eager, pressing, flexible, protean; here we are conscious of a searching and a selection, many potentialities and a choice of actualities, of a subconscient idea which is feeling around for its vital self-expression and shaping an instinctive action, — often, though in certain limits, with an unerring intuitive guidance of life to its immediate objective or to some yet distant purpose, — of a subconscient will too in the fibre of all this vast seeking and mutable impulsion. This too indeed works within limits, under fetters, in a given range of processes.

But when we get out into mind, Nature becomes there much more widely conscious of possibility and of choice; mind is aware of potentialities and of determinations in idea which are other than those of the immediate actuality or of the fixedly necessary consequence of the sum of past and present actualities; it is aware of numberless "may-be"s and "might-have-been"s, and these last are not entirely dead rejected things, but can return through the power of the Idea and effect future determinations and can fulfil themselves at last in the inner reality of their idea though, it may well be, in other forms and circumstances.

> *But is not man's conscious choice and will itself an instrument of the universal Nature, and is not his freedom an arbitrary illusion of his mentality which lives in each moment of the present and separates it by ignorance, by an abstraction of the mind from its determining past, so that he seems at every critical moment to exercise a free virgin choice, while all the time his choice is dominated by his own previous formations which he ignores?*

That is the first idea of Karma. Certainly, our present will must come in as one though not by any means the sole element of the act and formation, but in this view it is not a free ever-new will, but in the first place a child and birth of all the past nature, our action, our present Karma, the result of an already formed shape of the force of that nature, Swabhava. And in the second place our will is an instrument constantly shaped and used by something greater than ourselves. Only if there is a soul or self which is not a creation, but a master of Nature, not a formation of the stream of universal energy, but itself the former and creator of its own Karma, are we justified in our claim of an actual freedom or at least in our aspiration to a real liberty. There is the whole heart of the debate, the nodus and escape of this perplexed issue.

> *Is there no relation between man's subjection to the blind force of Karmic Necessity and his irrepressible impulse of freedom, between his earthly human nature at whirl in the machinery of mind, life and body and the master-Soul, the free Godhead, the real Man behind?*

The soul of man is a power of the self-existence which manifests the universe and not the creature and slave of a mechanical Nature; and it is only the natural instruments of his being, it is mind, life and body and their functions and members which are helpless apparatus and gear of the machinery. These things are subject to the action of Karma, but man in himself, the real man within is not its subject, *na karma lipyate nare.* Rather is Karma his instrument and its developments the material he uses, and he is using it always from life to life for the shaping of a limited and individual, which may be one day a divine and cosmic personality. For the eternal Spirit enjoys an absolute freedom. This freedom appears to us no doubt in a certain status, origin or background of all being as an unconditioned infinite of existence, but also it is in relation to the universe the freedom of an existence which displays an infinite of possibilities and has a power of shaping at will out of its own potentiality the harmonies of the cosmos. Man, too, may well be capable of a release, *mokṣa,* into the unconditioned Infinite by cessation of all action, mind and personality. But that is not the whole of the Spirit's absolute freedom; it is rather an incomplete liberty, since it endures only by its inaction. But the freedom of the Spirit is not so dependent; it can remain unimpaired in all this action of Karma and is not diminished or abrogated by the pouring of its energies into the whirl of the universe.

> *Some spiritual thinkers maintain that man cannot enjoy this double freedom because as man he is an individual being and therefore a thing in nature and entirely subject to Karma. To be free he must get away from individuality and nature and Karma, and then man no longer exists, there is only the unconditioned Infinite.*

But this is to assume that there is no power of spiritual individuality, but only a power of individuation in Nature. All is then a formation of a nodus of mental, vital and physical Karma with which the one self for a long time mistakenly identifies its being by the delusion of ego. But, if on the contrary, there is any such thing as an individual power of spirit, it must, in whatever degree of actuality, share in the united force and freedom of the self-existent Divinity; for it is being of his being.

Why is man bound by Karma and conditioned and determined by its law though he is free in spirit? Why does he not have complete freedom?

It is because there is separation between his outward nature and his inmost spiritual self and he does not live in that outwardness with his whole being, but with a shape, turn and mental formation of himself which he calls his ego or his personality. The cosmic Spirit in matter seems itself to be so bound, for the same reason. It has started an outward compressed action, a law and disposition of material energy which must be allowed to unroll its consequences; itself holds back behind and conceals its shaping touch; but still its supporting assent and impulse are there and these come out more into the open as Nature raises herself in the scales of life and mind. Neverthelsess, even in mind and even in its phenomenon of a conscious will Karma is the first law and there cannot be there a complete freedom; there is no such thing as a mental will which is absolutely free. And this is because mind is part of the action of the outward Ignorance, an action which seeks for knowledge but does not possess its full light and power, which can conceive of Self and Spirit and infinity and reflect them, but not altogether live in them, which can quiver with infinite possibility but can only deal in a limited half-effective fashion with restricted possibilities. An Ignorance cannot be permitted to have, even if in its nature it could have, free mastery. It would never do for an ignorant mind and will to be given a wide and real freedom; for it would upset the right order of the energy which the Spirit has set at work and produce a most unholy confusion. It must be forced to obey or, if it resists, to bear the reaction of the Law; its partial freedom of a clouded and stumbling knowledge must be constantly overruled both in its action and its result by the law of universal Nature and the will of the seeing universal Spirit who governs the dispositions and consequences of Karma. This constrained overruled action is in patent fact the character of our mental being and action.

XV

KARMA AND REBIRTH

The idea of Karma in ancient times was closely associated with a belief in rebirth. Is this association based on any inevitable necessity?

This close association between Karma and rebirth was not a mere accident, but a perfectly intelligible and indeed inevitable union of two related truths which are needed for each other's completeness and can with difficulty exist in separation. These two things are the soul side and the nature side of one and the same cosmic sequence. Rebirth is meaningless without Karma, and Karma has no fount of inevitable origin and no rational and no moral justification if it is not an instrumentality for the sequences of the soul's continuous experience.

Why is Karma necessary for rebirth?

If we believe that the soul is repeatedly reborn in the body, we must believe also that there is some link between the lives that preceded and the lives that follow and that the past of the soul has an effect on its future; and that is the spiritual essence of the law of Karma. To deny it would be to establish a reign of the most chaotic incoherence, such as we find only in the leaps and turns of the mind in dream or in the thoughts of madness, and hardly even there. And if this existence were, as the cosmic pessimist imagines, a dream or an illusion or, worse, as Schopenhauer would have it, a delirium and insanity of the soul, we might accept some such law of inconsequent consequence. But, taken even at its worst, this world of life differs from dream, illusion and madness by its plan of fine, complex and subtle sequences, the hanging together and utility even of its discords, the general and particular harmony of its relations, which, if they are not the harmony we would have, not our longed-for ideal harmony, has still at every point the stamp of a Wisdom and an Idea at work; it is not the act of a Mind in tatters or a machine in dislocation. The continuous existence of the soul in rebirth must signify an evolution if not of the self, for that is said to be immutable, yet of its more outward active soul or self of experience. This evolution is not possible if there is not a connected sequence from life to life, a result of action and experience, an evolutionary consequence to the soul, a law of Karma.

What is the necessity of rebirth to Karma?

If we give to Karma its integral and not a truncated meaning, we must admit rebirth for the sufficient field of its action.

What is the integral meaning of Karma, and why is rebirth necessary as a field of its working?

Karma is not quite the same thing as a material or substantial law of cause and effect, the antecedent and its mechanical consequence. That would perfectly admit of a Karma which could be carried on in time and the results come with certainty in their proper place, their just degree by a working out of the balance of forces, but need not in any way touch the human originator who might have passed away from the scene by the time the result of his acts got into manifestation. A mechanical Nature could well visit the sins of the fathers not on them, but on their fourth or their four-hundredth generation, as indeed this physical Nature does, and no objection of injustice or any other mental or moral objection could rise, for the only justice or reason of mechanism is that it shall work according to the law of its structure and the fixed eventuality of its force in action. We cannot demand from it a mind or a moral equity or any kind of supraphysical responsibility. The universal energy grinds out inconsciently its effects and individuals are only fortuitous or subordinate means of its workings; the soul itself, if there is a soul, makes only a part of the mechanism of Nature, exists not for itself, but as a utility for her business. But

Karma is more than a mechanical law of antecedent and consequence. Karma is action, there is a thing done and a doer and an active consequence; these three are the three joints, the three locks, the three *sandhis* of the connexus of Karma. And it is a complex mental, moral and physical working; for the law of it is not less true of the mental and moral than of the physical consequence of the act to the doer. The will and the idea are the driving force of the action, and the momentum does not come from some commotion in my chemical atoms or some working of ion and electron or some weird biological effervescence. Therefore the act and consequence must have some relation to the will and the idea and there must be a mental and moral consequence to the soul which has the will and idea. That, if we admit the individual as a real being, signifies a continuity of act and consequence to him and therefore rebirth for a field of this working. It is evident that in one life we do not and cannot labour out and exhaust all the values and powers of that life, but only carry on a past threat, weave out something in the present, prepare infinitely more for the future.

Is not the existence of the individual soul implied in the idea of rebirth? Would the consequence of rebirth follow from the very nature of Karma if there were only an All-Soul of the universe?

It would not, because then it would be that which is carrying on in myriads of forms its past, working out some present result, spinning yarn of Karma for a future weft of the consequence. It is the All-Soul which would be the originator, would upbear the force of the act, would receive and exhaust or again take up for farther uses the returning force of the consequence. Nothing essential would depend on its doing all these things through the same individual mask of its being. For the individual would only be a prolonged moment of the All-Soul, and what it originated in this moment of its being which I call myself, might very well produce its result on some other moment of the same being which from the point of view of my ego would be somebody quite different from and unconnected with myself. There would be no injustice, no unreason in such an apparently vicarious reaping of the fruit or suffering of the consequence; for what has a mask, though it be a living and suffering mask, to do with these things? And, in fact, in the nature of life in the material universe a working out of the result of the action of one in the lives of many others, an effect of the individual's action on the group or the whole is everywhere the law. What I sow in this hour is reaped by my posterity for several generations and we can then call it the Karma of the family. What the men of today and community or people resolve upon and execute, comes back with a blessing or a sword upon the future of their race when they themselves have passed away and are no longer there to rejoice or to suffer; and that we can speak of as the Karma of the nation. Mankind as a whole too has a Karma; what it wrought in its past will shape its future destiny; individuals seem only to be temporary units of human thought, will, nature who act according to the compulsion of the soul in humanity and disappear; but the Karma of the race which they have helped to form continues through the centuries, the millenniums, the cycles.

But we can see, when we look into ourselves, that this relation of the individual to the whole has a different significance; it does not mean that I have no existence except as a more or less protracted moment in the cosmic becoming of the All-Soul; that too is only a superficial appearance and much subtler and greater is the truth of my being.

What then is the real truth of the individual soul and what is its proper relation to the All-Soul or the cosmic spirit?

The original and eternal Reality, the Alpha and Omega, the Godhead is neither separate in the individual nor is he only and solely a Pantheos, a cosmic spirit. He is at once the eternal individual and the eternal All-Soul of this and many universes, and at the same time he is much more than these things. This universe might end, but he would still be; and I too, though the universe might end, could still exist in him; and all these eternal souls would still exist in him. But as his being is for ever, so the succession of his creations too is for ever; if one creation were to come to an end, it would be only that another might begin and the new would carry on with a fresh commencement and initiation the possibility that had not been worked out in the old, for there can be no end to the self-manifestation of the Infinite. *Nāsti anto vistarasya me.* The universe finds itself in me, even as I find myself in the universe, because we are this face and that face of the one eternal Reality, and individual being is as much needed as universal being to work out this manifestation. The individual vision of things is as true as the universal vision, both are ways of the self-seeing of the Eternal. I may now see myself as a creature contained in the universe, but when I come to self-knowledge, I see too the universe to be a thing contained in myself, subtly by implication in my individuality, amply in the great universalised self I then become. These are data of an ancient experience, things known and voiced of old, though they may seem shadowy and transcendental to the positive modern mind which has long pored so minutely on outward things that it has become dazed and blind to any greater light and is only slowly recovering the power to see through its folds; but they are for all that always valid and can be experienced today by any one of us who chooses to turn to the deepest way of the inner experience. Modern thought and science, if we look at the new knowledge given us in its whole, do not contradict them, but only trace for us the outward effect and workings of these realities; for always we find in the end that truth of self is not contradicted, but reproduced and made effectual here by law of Energy and law of Matter.

Though the truth of the individual soul has to be admitted in considering rebirth, is it not necessary to guard against the ancient tendency of over-emphasising its importance?

The old idea of rebirth erred by an excessive individualism.

Too self-concentrated, it treated one's rebirth and Karma as too much one's own single affair, a sharply separate movement in the whole, leaned too much on one's own concern with one's self and, even while it admitted universal relations and a unity with the whole, yet taught the human being to see in life principally a condition and means of his own spiritual benefit and separate salvation. That came from the view of the universe as a movement which proceeds out of something beyond, something from which each being enters into life and returns out of it to its source, and the absorbing idea of that return as the one thing that at all matters. Our being in the world, so treated, came in the end to be regarded as an episode and in sum and essence an unhappy and discreditable episode in the changeless eternity of the Spirit. But this was too summary a view of the will and the ways of the Spirit in existence. Certain it is that while we are here, our rebirth or Karma even while it runs on its own lines, is intimately one with the same lines in the universal existence. But my self-knowledge and self-finding do not abolish my oneness with other life and other beings. An intimate universality is part of the glory of spiritual perfection. This idea of universality, of oneness not only with God or the eternal Self in me, but with all humanity and other beings, is growing to be the most prominent strain in our minds and it has to be taken more largely into account in any future idea or computation of the significance of rebirth and Karma. It was admitted in old times; the Buddhist law of compassion was a recognition of its importance; but it has to be given a still more pervading power in the general significance.

XVI

KARMA AND JUSTICE

It is a common belief that according to the law of Karma a man's actions in one life determine the nature, circumstances and happenings of his next life. If the sum of past actions was good, the life in the next birth is successful, prosperous and happy; if bad, the next life is unsuccessful, unhappy, full of suffering and misfortune. Is there any truth in this belief?

These are very summary popular notions and offer no foothold to the philosophic reason and no answer to a search for the true significance of life. A vast world system which serves only as a school of sin and virtue and consists of a system of rewards and whippings, does not make any appeal to our intelligence. The soul or spirit within us, if it is divine, immortal or celestial, cannot be sent here solely to be put to school for this kind of crude and primitive moral education; if it enters into the Ignorance, it must be because there is some larger principle or possibility of its being that has to be worked out through the Ignorance. If, on the other hand, it is a being from the Infinite plunged for some cosmic purpose into the obscurity of Matter and growing to self-knowledge within it, its life here and the significance of that life must be something more than that of an infant coddled and whipped into virtuous ways; it must be a growth out of an assumed ignorance towards its own full spiritual stature with a final passage into an immortal consciousness, knowledge, strength, beauty, divine purity and power, and for such a spiritual growth this law of Karma is all too puerile. Even if the soul is something created, an infant being that has to learn from Nature and grow into immortality, it must be by a larger law of growth and not by some divine code of primitive and barbaric justice. This idea of Karma is a construction of the smaller part of the human vital mind concerned with its petty rules of life and its desires and joys and sorrows and erecting their puny standards into the law and aim of the cosmos. These notions cannot be acceptable to the thinking mind; they have too evidently the stamp of a construction fashioned by our human ignorance.

Is the soul then not governed by this Karmic law which is supposed to reward it for its virtues in past lives and inflict suffering for its sins? Are not the results of a man's actions in his past lives visited on him in his present life?

It is not conceivable that the spirit within is an automaton in the hands of Karma, a slave in this life of its past action; the truth must be less rigid and more plastic. If a certain amount of results of past Karma is formulated in the present life, it must be with the consent of the psychic being which presides over the new formation of its earth-experience and assents not merely to an outward compulsory process, but to a secret Will and Guidance. That secret Will is not mechanical, but spiritual; the guidance comes from an Intelligence which may use mechanical processes but is not their subject. Self-expression and experience are what the soul seeks by its birth into the body; whatever is necessary for the self-expression and experience of this life, whether it intervenes as an automatic outcome of past lives or as a free selection of results and a continuity or as a new development, whatever is a means of creation of the future, that will be formulated: for the principle is not the working out of a mechanism of Law, but the development of the nature through cosmic experience so that eventually it may grow out of the Ignorance. There must therefore be two elements, Karma as an instrument, but also the secret Consciousness and Will within working through the mind, life and body as the user. Fate, whether purely mechanical or created by ourselves, a chain of our own manufacture, is only one factor of existence; Being and its consciousness and its will are a still more important factor. In Indian astrology which considers all life circumstances to be Karma, mostly predetermined or indicated in the graph of the stars, there is still provision made for the energy and force of the being which can change or cancel part or much of what is so written or even all but the most imperative and powerful bindings of Karma. This is a reasonable account of the balance: but there is also to be added to the computation the fact that destiny is not simple but complex; the destiny which binds our physical being, binds it so long or in so far as a greater law does not intervene. Action belongs to the physical part of us, it is the physical outcome of our being; but behind our surface is a freer life power, a freer mind power which has another energy and can create another destiny and bring it in to modify the primary plan, and when the soul and self emerge, when we become consciously spiritual beings, that change can cancel or wholly remodel the graph of our physical fate. Karma, then, — or at least any mechanical law of Karma, — cannot be accepted as the sole determinant of circumstances and the whole machinery of rebirth and of our future evolution.

What is the explanation of the sudden strokes of luck or fortune which are quite frequent phenomena in life? The popular belief is that they are rewards for the forgotten good actions of the past life. Similarly, apparently inexplicable strokes of bad fortune are taken to be the results of sins committed in the past life. Is there some truth in this belief?

There is indeed in our life a very large element of what we call luck or fortune, which baulks our effort of result or gives the prize without effort or to an inferior energy: the secret cause of these caprices of Destiny — or causes, for the roots of Fortune may be manifold, — must be no doubt partly sought for in our hidden past; but it is difficult to accept the simple solution that good luck is return for a forgotten virtuous action in a past life and bad luck a return for a sin or crime. If we see the righteous man suffering here, it is difficult to believe that this paragon of virtue was in the last life a scoundrel and is paying, even after his exemplary conversion by a new birth, for sins he then committed; nor, if the wicked triumphs, can we easily suppose that he was in his last life a saint who has suddenly taken a wrong turn but continues to receive a cash return for his previous virtue. A total change of this kind between life and life is possible though not likely to be frequent, but to saddle the new opposite personality with the rewards or punishments of the old looks like a purposeless and purely mechanical procedure. This and many other difficulties arise, and the too simple logic of the correlation is not so strong as it claims to be; the idea of retribution of Karma as a compensation for the injustice of life and Nature is a feeble basis for the theory, for it puts forward a shallow and superficial human feeling and standard as the sense of the cosmic Law and is based on an unsound reasoning; there must be some other and stronger foundation for the law of Karma.

Is there no truth then in this theory of Karma which looks for vital-hedonistic returns for ethical actions and imposes that as the sole meaning of the universal Law of Karma?

A partial truth of fact, not of fundamental or general principle, may be admitted for this doctrine; for although the lines of the action of energy are distinct and independent, they can act together and upon each other, though not by any rigidly fixed law of correspondence.

It is possible that in the total method of the returns of Nature there intervenes a strand of connection or rather interaction between vital-physical good and ill and ethical good and ill, a limited correspondence and meeting-point between divergent dualities not amounting to an inseparable coherence. Our own varying energies, desires, movements are mixed together in their working and can bring about a mixed result: our vital part does demand substantial and external rewards for virtue, for knowledge, for every intellectual, aesthetic, moral or physical effort; it believes firmly in punishment for sin and even for ignorance. This may well either create or else reply to a corresponding cosmic action; for Nature takes us as we are and to some extent suits her movements to our need or our demands on her. If we accept the action of invisible Forces upon us, there may be also invisible Forces in Life-Nature that belong to the same plane of Consciousness-Force as this part of our being, Forces that move according to the same plan or the same power-motive as our lower vital nature. It can be often observed that when a self-assertive vital egoism goes on trampling on its way without restraint or scruple all that opposes its will or desire, it raises a mass of reactions against itself, reactions of hatred, antagonism, unease in men which may have their result now or hereafter, and still more formidable adverse reactions in universal Nature. It is as if the patience of Nature, her willingness to be used were exhausted; the very forces that the ego of the strong vital man seized and bent to its purpose rebel and turn against him; those he had trampled on rise up and receive power for his downfall; the insolent vital force of Man strikes against the throne of Necessity and is dashed to pieces or the lame foot of Punishment reaches at last the successful offender. This reaction to his energies may come upon him in another life and not at once, it may be a burden of consequence he takes up in his return to the field of these Forces; it may happen on a small as well as a large scale, to the small vital being and his small errors as well as in these larger instances. For the principle will be the same; the mental being in us seeking for success by a misuse of force which Nature admits but reacts in the end against it, receives the adverse return in the guise of defeat and suffering and failure. But the promotion of this minor line of causes and results to the status of an invariable absolute Law or the whole cosmic rule of action of a supreme Being is not valid; they belong to a middle region between the inmost or supreme Truth of things and the impartiality of material Nature.

What is then the essential meaning and purpose of the complex working of the law of Karma? What is its fundamental significance for our spiritual evolution on earth?

The reactions of Nature are not in essence meant as reward or punishment; that is not their fundamental value, which is rather an inherent value of natural relations and, in so far as it affects the spiritual evolution, a value of the lessons of experience in the soul's cosmic training. If we touch fire, it burns, but there is no principle of punishment in this relation of cause and effect, it is a lesson of relation and a lesson of experience; so in all Nature's dealings with us there is a relation of things and there is a corresponding lesson of experience. The action of the cosmic Energy is complex and the same Forces may act in different ways according to circumstances, to the need of the being, to the intention of the cosmic Power in its action; our life is affected not only by its own energies but by the energies of others and by universal Forces, and all this vast interplay cannot be determined in its results solely by the one factor of an all-governing moral law and its exclusive attention to the merits and demerits, the sins and virtues of individual human beings. Nor can good fortune and evil fortune, pleasure and pain, happiness and misery and suffering be taken as if they existed merely as incentives and deterrents to the natural being in its choice of good and evil. It is for experience, for growth of the individual being that the soul enters into rebirth; joy and grief, pain and suffering, fortune and misfortune are parts of that experience, means of that growth: even the soul may of itself accept or choose poverty, misfortune and suffering as helpful to its growth, stimulants of a rapid development, and reject riches of prosperity and success as dangerous and conducive to a relaxation of its spiritual effort. Happiness and success bringing happiness are, no doubt, a legitimate demand of humanity; it is an attempt of Life and Matter to catch a pale reflection or a gross image of felicity, but a superficial happiness and material success, however desirable to our vital nature, are not the main object of our existence; if that had been the intention, life would have been otherwise arranged in the cosmic ordinance of things. All the secret of the circumstances of rebirth centres around the one capital need of the soul, the need of growth, the need of experience; that governs the line of its evolution and all the rest is accessory. Cosmic existence is not a vast administrative system of universal justice with a cosmic Law of recompense and retribution as its machinery or a divine Legislator and Judge at its centre. It is seen by us first as a great automatic movement of energy of Nature, and in it emerges a self-developing movement of consciousness, a movement therefore of Spirit working out its own being in the motion of energy of Nature. In this motion takes place the cycle of rebirth, and in that cycle the soul, the psychic being, prepares for itself, — or the Divine Wisdom or the cosmic Consciousness-Force prepares for it and through its action, — whatever is needed for the next step in its evolution, the next formation of personality, the coming nexus of necessary experiences constantly provided and organised out of the continuous flux of past, present and future energies for each new birth, for each new step of the Spirit backward or forward or else still in a circle, but always a step in the growth of the being towards its destined self-unfolding in Nature.

XVII

KARMA AND MORALITY

Since the vital-hedonistic interpretation of the law of Karma, whether applied to the present life or extended to future births, is only a reflection of the lower ethical mind of humanity, there should be a higher line of the law of Karma corresponding to our higher ethical aspiration. What is the essential difference between this lower and the higher ethical aspiration?

The higher ethical mind no longer follows good for a reward now on earth or in another existence, but for the sake of good, and no longer shuns evil for fear of punishment on earth later on in this life or else in another life or in hell, but because to follow evil is a degradation and affliction of its being and a fall from its innate and imperative endeavour. This is to it a necessity of its moral nature, a truly categorical imperative, a call that in the total more complex nature of man may be dulled or suppressed or excluded by the claim of its other parts and their needs, but to the ethical mind is binding and absolute. The virtue that demands a reward for acting well and needs a penalty to keep it walking in the straight way is no real portion, no true law of the ethical being, but rather a mixed creation, a rule of his practical reason that seeks always after utility and holds that to be right which is helpful and expedient, a rule that looks first not at the growth of the soul but at the mechanical securing of a regulated outward conduct and to secure it, bribes and terrifies the vital being into acquiescence and a reluctant subordination of its own instincts and natural ventures. The virtue so created is an expedience, a social decency, a prudent limitation of egoism, a commercial substitute for the true thing; or, at best, it is a habit of the mind and not a truth of the soul, and in the mind a fabrication, mixed and of inferior stuff, a conventional virtue, insecure, destructible by the wear and tear of life, easily confused with other expediencies or purchasable or conquerable by them, — it is not a high and clear upbuilding, an enduring and inwardly living self-creation of the soul.

Is conventional morality a part of the higher ethical trend of humanity or a result of its lower and limited expression? Does it not help the progress of humanity by exercising a stabilising influence over the unruly elements in our nature?

Whatever its practical utility or service as a step of the transition, the mental habit of confusion and vitalistic compromise it fosters and the more questionable confusions and compromises that habit favours, have made conventional morality one of the chief of the forces that hold back human life from progressing to a true ethical order. If humanity has made any lasting and true advance, it has been not through the virtue created by reward and punishment or any of the conventional sanctions powerful on the little vital ego, but by an insistence from the higher mind on the lower, an insistence on right for its own sake, on imperative moral values, on an absolute law and truth of ethical being and ethical conduct that must be obeyed whatever the recalcitrances of the lower mind, whatever the pains of the vital problem, whatever the external result, the inferior issue.

But is not this higher ethical tendency, which discards all other standards and exclusively follows virtue for its own sake, itself an exaggerated and extremist tendency making for rigidity and narrowness and often retarding and even opposing the progressive movement of life and soul?

This kind of high absoluteness in the ethical demand is appalling to the flesh and the ego, for it admits of no comfortable indulgence and compromise, no abating reserves or conditions, no profitable compact between the egoistic life and virtue. It is offensive too to the practical reason, for it ignores the complexity of the world and of human nature and seems to savour of an extremism and exclusive exaggeration as dangerous to life as it is exalted in ideal purpose. *Fiat justitia ruat coelum,* let justice and right be done though the heavens fall, is a rule of conduct that only the ideal mind can accept with equanimity or the ideal life tolerate in practice. And even to the larger ideal mind this absoluteness becomes untrustworthy if it is an obedience not to the higher law of the soul, but to an outward moral law, a code of conduct. For then in place of a lifting enthusiasm we have the rigidity of the Pharisee, a puritan fierceness or narrowness or the life-killing tyranny of a single insufficient side of the nature. This is not yet that higher mental movement, but a straining towards it, an attempt to rise above the transitional law and the vitalistic compromise. And it brings with it an artificiality, a tension, a coercion, often a repellent austerity which, disregarding as it does sanity and large wisdom and the simple naturalness of the true ethical mind and the flexibilies of life, tyrannising over but not transforming it, is not the higher perfection of our nature.

What is then the real value of this absolutist ethical tendency of our higher mind in the progressive perfection of our soul and nature? How can this tendency achieve its true fulfilment?

There is here the feeling after a great output of moral energy, an attempt well worth making, if the aim can indeed so be accomplished, to build up by the insistence on a rigid obedience to a law of moral action that which is yet non-existent or imperfectly existent in us but which alone can make the law of our conduct a thing true and living, — an ethical being with an inalienably ethical nature. No rule imposed on him from outside, whether in the name of a supposed mechanical or impersonal law or of God or prophet, can be, as such, true or right or binding on man: it becomes that only when it answers to some demand or aids some evolution of his inner being. And when that inner being is revealed, evolved, at each moment naturally active, simply and spontaneously imperative, then we get the true, the inner and intuitive Law in its light of self-knowledge, its beauty of self-fulfilment, its intimate life-significance. An act of justice, truth, love, compassion, purity, sacrifice becomes then the faultless expression, the natural outflowering of our soul of justice, our soul of truth, our soul of love and compassion, our soul of purity or sacrifice. And before the greatness of its imperative mandate to the outer nature the vital being and the practical reason and surface seeking intelligence must and do bow down as before something greater than themselves, something that belongs directly to the divine and the infinite.

What is the nature and significance of the working of the law of Karma corresponding to this higher ethical trend of human nature?

It is here that we get the clue to the higher law of Karma, of the output and returns of energy, and see it immediately and directly to be, what all law of Karma, really and ultimately, if at first covertly, is for man, a law of his spiritual evolution. The true return to the act of virtue, to the ethically right output of his energy, — his reward, if you will, and the sole recompense on which he has a right to insist, — is its return upon him in a growth of the moral strength within him, an upbuilding of his ethical being, a flowering of the soul of right, justice, love, compassion, purity, truth, strength, courage, self-giving that he seeks to be. The true return to the act of evil, to the ethically wrong output of energy, — his punishment, if you will, and the sole penalty he has any need or right to fear, — is its return upon him in a retardation of the growth, a demolition of the upbuilding, an obscuration, tarnishing, impoverishing of the soul, of the pure, strong and luminous being that he is striving to be. An inner happiness he may gain by his act, the calm, peace, satisfaction of the soul fulfilled in right, or an inner calamity, the suffering, disturbance, unease and malady of its descent or failure, but he can demand from God or moral Law no other. The ethical soul, — not the counterfeit but the real, — accepts the pains and sufferings and difficulties and fierce intimidations of life, not as a punishment for its sins, but as an opportunity and trial, an opportunity for its growth, a trial of its built or native strength, and good fortune and all outer success not as a coveted reward of virtue, but as an opportunity also and an even greater more difficult trial. What to this high seeker of Right can mean the vital law of Karma or what can its gods do to him that he can fear or long for? The ethical-vitalistic explanation of the world and its meaning and measures has for such a soul, for man at this height of his evolution no significance. He has travelled beyond the jurisdiction of the Powers of the middle air, the head of his spirit's endeavour is lifted above the dull gray-white belt that is their empire.

XVIII

THE PURSUIT OF KNOWLEDGE

As in the seeking for moral good, so in the seeking for knowledge, the modern mind has laid predominant stress on its practical or utilitarian value. Can this be taken as its right motive and aim?

Mind in its first action pursues knowledge with a certain curiosity, but turns it mainly to practical experience, to a help that enables it to fulfil better and to increase more assuredly the first uses and purposes of life. Afterwards it evolves a freer use of the intelligence, but there is still a dominant turn towards the vital purpose. But the higher mind of humanity is no more content with a utilitarian use of knowledge as its last word in the seeking of the intelligence than with a vitalistic and utilitarian turn and demand of the ethical being. As in the ethical, so in the intellectual being of man there emerges a necessity of knowledge which is no longer its utility for life, its need of knowing rightly in order to act rightly, to deal successfully and intelligently with the world around it, but a necessity of the soul, an imperative demand of the inner being.

What should be the true aim of the pursuit of knowledge?

The pursuit of knowledge for the sake of knowledge is the true, the intrinsic *dharma* of the intellect and not for the sake primarily or even necessarily at all for the securing or the enlargement of the means of life and success in action. The vital kinetic man tends indeed to regard this passion of the intellect as a respectable but still rather unpractical and often trivial curiosity: as he values ethics for its social effects or for its rewards in life, so he values knowledge for its external helpfulness; science is great in his eyes because of its inventions, its increase of comforts and means and appliances: his standard in all things is vital efficiency. But, in fact, nature sees and stirs from the first to a larger amd more inward Will and is moved with a greater purpose, and all seeking for knowledge springs from a necessity of the mind, a necessity of its nature, and that means a necessity of the soul that is here in nature. Its need to know is one with its need to grow, and from the eager curiosity of the child upward to the serious stress of mind of the thinker, scholar, scientist, philosopher, the fundamental purpose of Nature, the constant in it, is the same. All the time that she seems busy only with the maintenance of her works, with life, with the outward, her secret underlying purpose is other, — it is the evolution of that which is hidden within her: for if her first dynamic word is life, her greater revealing word is consciousness and the evolution of life and action only the means of the evolution of the consciousness involved in life, the imprisoned soul, the Jiva. Action is a means, but knowledge is the sign and the growth of the conscious soul is the purpose. Man's use of the intelligence for the pursuit of knowledge is therefore that which distinguishes him most from other beings and gives him his high peculiar place in the scale of existence. His passion for knowledge, first world-knowledge, but afterwards self-knowledge and that in which both meet and find their common secret, God-knowledge, is the central drift of his ideal mind and a greater imperative of his being than that of action, though later in laying its complete hold on him, greater in the wideness of its reach and greater too in its effectiveness upon action, in the return of the world energy to his effectiveness upon action, in the return of the world energy to his power of the truth within him.

> *At what stage in man's evolution does this true aim become the ruling motive of his mind and the lower aim of utility fall away?*

It is when his mind is preparing to disengage itself, its pure self of will and intelligence, the radiant head of its endeavour from subjection to the vital motive that this imperative of nature, this intrinsic need that creates in the mind of man the urge towards knowledge, becomes something much greater, becomes instead more and more plainly the ideal absolute imperative of the soul emerging from the husks and sheaths of ignorance and pushing towards the truth, towards the light as the condition of its fulfilment and the very call of the Divine upon its being. The lure of an external utility ceases to be at all needed as an incentive towards knowledge, just as the lure of a vital reward offered now or hereafter ceases on the same high level of our ascent to be needed as an incentive to virtue, and to attach importance to it under whatever specious colour is even felt to be a degradation of the disinterestedness, a fall from the high purity of the soul motive. Already even in the more outward forms of intellectual seeking something of this absoluteness begins to be felt and to reign. The scientist pursues his discoveries in order that he may know the law and truth of the process of the universe and their practical results are only a secondary motive of the enquiring mind and no motive at all to the higher scientific intelligence. The philosopher is driven from within to search for the ultimate truth of things for the one sake of Truth only and all else but to see the very face of Truth becomes to him, to his absorbing mind and soul of knowledge, secondary or of no importance; nothing can be allowed to interfere with that one imperative. And there is the tendency to the same kind of exclusiveness in the interest and the process of this absolute. The thinker is concerned to seek out and enforce the truth on himself and the world regardless of any effect it may have in disturbing the established bases of life, religion, ethics, society, regardless of any other consideration whatsoever; he must express the word of the Truth whatever its dynamic results on life. And this absolute becomes most absolute, this imperative most imperative when the inner action surpasses the strong coldness of intellectual search and becomes a fiery striving for truth experience, a luminous inner truth living, a birth into a new truth consciousness. The enamoured of light, the sage, the Yogin of knowledge, the seer, the Rishi live for knowledge and in knowledge, because it is the absolute of light and truth that they seek after and its claim on them is single and absolute.

But though the real seeker of truth does not care for any material reward, there must be some return for the output of his mental energy in the economy of Nature. What is his benefit or gain from the pure pursuit of truth?

This also is a line of the world energy, — for the world Shakti is a Shakti of consciousness and knowledge and not only a Power of force and action, — and the output of the energy of knowledge brings its results as surely as the energy of the will seeking after success in action or after right ethical conduct. But the result that it brings on this higher plane of the seeking in mind is simply and purely the upward growth of the soul in light and truth; that and whatever happiness it brings is the one supreme reward demanded by the soul of knowledge and the darkening of the light within, the pain of the fall from truth, the pain of the imperfection of not living only by its law and wholly in the light is its one penalty of suffering. The outward rewards and the sufferings of life are small things to the higher soul of knowledge in man: even his high mind of knowledge will often face all that the world can do to afflict it, just as it is ready to make all manner of sacrifices in the pursuit and the affirmation of the truth it knows and lives for. Bruno burning in the Roman fire, the martyrs of all religions suffering and welcoming as witnesses to the light within them torture and persecution, Buddha leaving all to discover the dark cause of universal suffering in this world of the impermanence and the way of escape into the supreme Permanence, the ascetic casting away as an illusion life in the world and its activities, enjoyments, attractions with the one will to enter into the absolute truth and the supreme consciousness are witnesses to this imperative of knowledge, its extreme examples and exponents.

Is it not a fact that the pursuit of practical knowledge brings better returns in life than the pursuit of moral right?

As a power for the returns of life the world energy seems to attach a more direct importance and give more tangible results to knowledge, to the right practical workings of the intelligence than it yields to moral right. In this material world it is at least doubtful how far moral good is repaid by vital good and moral evil punished by a recoil, but it is certain that we do pay very usually for our errors, for stupidity, for ignorance of the right way of action, for any ignoring or misapplication of the laws that govern our psychical, vital and physical being; it is certain that knowledge is a power for life efficiency and success. Intelligence pays its way in the material world, guards itself against vital and physical suffering, secures its vital rewards more surely than moral right and ethical purpose.

Through all these various motives for the pursuit of truth, does not Nature work out some intention which is fulfilled in her highest working? What is that intention?

The intention of Nature, the spiritual justification of her ways appears at last in the final turn of her energies leading the conscious soul along the lines of truth and knowledge. At first she is physical Nature building her firm field according to a base of settled truth and law but determined by a subconscient knowledge she does not yet share with her creatures. Next she is Life growing slowly self-conscious, seeking out knowledge that she may move seeingly in them along her ways and increase at once the complexity and the efficacy of her movements, but developing slowly too the consciousness that knowledge must be pursued for a higher and purer end, for truth, for the satisfaction, as the life expression and as the spiritual self-finding of the soul of knowledge. But, last, it is that soul itself growing in the truth and light, growing into the absolute truth of itself which is its perfection, that becomes the law and high end of her energies. And at each stage she gives returns according to the development of the aim and consciousness of the being. At first there is the return of skill and effectual intelligence, — and her own need explains sufficiently why she gives the rewards of life not, as the ethical mind in us would have it, to the just, not chiefly to moral good, but to the skilful and to the strong, to will and force and intelligence, — and then, more and more clearly disengaged, the return of enlightenment and the satisfaction of the mind and the soul in the conscious use and wise direction of its powers and capacities and, last of all, the one supreme return, the increase of the soul in light, the satisfaction of its perfection in knowledge, its birth into the highest consciousness and the pure fulfilment of its own innate imperative. It is that growth, a divine birth or spiritual self-exceeding its supreme reward, which for the Eastern mind has been always the highest gain, — the growth out of human ignorance into divine self-knowledge.

XIX

SUBJECTIVISM AND OBJECTIVISM (1)

The modern mind, which is largely a product of the materialistic and utilitarian intellectualism of the nineteenth century, has been dominated by its objective view of life. What is the essential meaning of objectivism and what are its practical consequences when it is taken to be the governing law of individual and social existence?

Objectivism proceeds by the analytical reason and takes an external mechanical view of the whole of existence. It looks at the world as a thing, an object, a process to be studied by an observing reason which places itself abstractly outside the elements and the sum of what it has to consider and observes it thus from outside as one would an intricate mechanism. The laws of this process are considered as so many mechanical rules or settled forces acting upon the individual or the group which, when they have been observed and distinguished by the reason, have by one's will or by some will to be organised and applied fully much as Science applies the laws it discovers. These laws or rules have to be imposed on the individual by his own abstract reason and will isolated as a ruling authority from his other parts or by the reason and will of other individuals or of the group, and they have to be imposed on the group itself either by its own collective reason and will embodied in some machinery of control which the mind considers as something apart from the life of the group or by the reason and will of some other group external to it or of which it is in some way a part. So the State is viewed in modern political thought as an entity in itself, as if it were something apart from the community and its individuals, something which has the right to impose itself on them and control them in the fulfilment of some idea of right, good or interest which is inflicted on them by a restraining and fashioning power rather than developed in them and by them as a thing towards which their self and nature are impelled to grow. Life is to be managed, harmonised, perfected by an adjustment, a manipulation, a machinery through which it is passed and by which it is shaped. A law outside oneself, — outside even when it is discovered or determined by the individual reason and accepted or enforced by the individual will, — this is the governing idea of objectivism; a mechanical process of management, ordering, perfection, this is its conception of practice.

What is the central difference, between subjectivism and objectivism in their viewpoints and their dynamic consequences in life?

Subjectivism proceeds from within and regards everything from the point of view of a containing and developing self-consciousness. The law here is within ourselves; life a self-creating process, a growth and development at first subconscious, then half-conscious and at last more and more fully conscious of that which we are potentially and hold within ourselves; the principle of its progress is an increasing self-recognition, self-realisation and a resultant self-shaping. Reason and will are only effective movements of the self, reason a process in self-recognition, will a force for self-affirmation and self-shaping. Moreover, reason and intellectual will are only a part of the means by which we recognise and realise ourselves. Subjectivism tends to take a large and complex view of our nature and being and to recognise many powers of knowledge, many forces of effectuation. Even, we see it, in its first movement away from the external and objective method, discount and belittle the importance of the work of the reason and assert the supremacy of the life-impulse or the essential Will-to-be in opposition to the claims of the intellect or else affirm some deeper power of knowledge, called nowadays the intuition, which sees things in the whole, in their truth, in their profundities and harmonies, while intellectual reason breaks up, falsifies, affirms superficial appearances and harmonises only by a mechanical adjustment. But substantially we can see that what is meant by this intuition is the self-consciousness, feeling, perceiving, grasping in its substance and aspects rather than analysing in its mechanism its own truth and nature and powers. The whole impulse of subjectivism is to get at the self, to live in the self, to see by the self, to live out the truth of the self internally and externally but always from an internal initiation and centre.

Is it not likely that subjectivism in its search for the true self may stop short of the complete discovery and may attach itself to some of its incomplete or subsidiary aspects? What is the final aim at which the progressive endeavour of subjective seeking is intended to arrive?

The subjective search for the self may, like the objective, lean preponderantly to identification with the conscious physical life, because the body is or seems to be the frame and determinant here of the mental and vital movements and capacities. Or it may identify itself with the vital being, the life-soul in us and its emotions, desires, impulses, seekings for power and growth and egoistic fulfilment. Or it may rise to a conception of man as a mental and moral being, exalt to the first place his inner growth, power and perfection, individual and collective, and set it before us as the true aim of existence. A sort of subjective materialism, pragmatic and outwardgoing, is a possible standpoint; but in this the subjective tendency cannot linger long. For its natural impulse is to go always inward and it only begins to feel itself and have satisfaction of itself when it gets to the full conscious life within and feels all its power, joy and forceful potentiality pressing for fulfilment. Man at this stage regards himself as a profound, vital Will-to-be which uses body as its instrument and to which the powers of mind are servants and ministers. This is the cast of that vitalism which in various striking forms has played recently so great a part and still exercises a considerable influence on human thought. Beyond it we get to a subjective idealism now beginning to emerge and become prominent, which seeks the fulfilment of man in the satisfaction of his inmost religious, aesthetic, ethical, intuitive, his highest intellectual and ethical, his deepest sympathetic and emotional nature and, regarding this as the fullness of our being and the whole object of our being, tries to subject to it the physical and vital existence. These come to be considered rather as a possible symbol and instrument of the subjective life flowing out into forms than as having any value in themselves. A certain tendency to mysticism, occultism and the search for a self independent of the life and the body accompanies this new movement — new to modern life after the reign of individualism and objective intellectualism — and emphasises its real trend and character.

But here also it is possible for subjectivism to go beyond and to discover the true Self as something greater even than mind. Mind, life and body then become merely an instrumentation for the increasing expression of this Self in the world, — instruments not equal in their hierarchy, but equal in their necessity to the whole, so that their complete perfection and harmony and unity as elements of our self-expression become essential to the true aim of our living. And yet that aim would not be to perfect life, body and mind in themselves, but to develop them so as to make a fit basis for the revelation in our inner and outer life of the luminous Self, the secret Godhead who is one and yet various in all of us, in every being and existence, thing and creature. The ideal of human existence personal and social would be its progressive transformation into a conscious outflowering of the joy, power, love, light, beauty of the transcendent and universal Spirit.

XX

SUBJECTIVISM AND OBJECTIVISM (2)

What were the principal effects of the vital subjectivism to which the modern mind arrived in its recoil from the intellectual objectivism of the nineteenth century and which very strongly influenced not only its philosophy, art and religion but also its political and social life?

After the material formula which governed the greater part of the nineteenth century had burdened man with the heaviest servitude to the machinery of the outer material life that he has ever yet been called upon to bear, the first attempt to break through, to get to the living reality in things and away from the mechanical idea of life and living and society, landed us in that surface vitalism which had already begun to govern thought before the two formulas inextricably locked together lit up and flung themselves on the lurid pyre of the World War. The vital élan brought us no deliverance, but only used the machinery already created with a more feverish insistence, a vehement attempt to live more rapidly, more intensely, an inordinate will to act and to succeed, to enlarge the mere force of living, to pile up a gigantic efficiency of life.

But could this adverse result not have been averted if the vital subjectivism had taken a profound and complete form instead of remaining shallow and incomplete?

It could not have been otherwise even if this vitalism had been less superficial and external, more truly subjective. To live, to act, to grow, to increase the vital force, to understand, utilise and fulfil the intuitive impulse of life are not things evil in themselves: rather they are excellent things, if rightly followed and rightly used, that is to say, if they are directed to something beyond the mere vitalistic impulse and are governed by that within which is higher than Life. The Life-power is an instrument, not an aim; it is in the upward scale the first great subjective supraphysical instrument of the Spirit and the base of all action and endeavour. But a Life-power that sees nothing beyond itself, nothing to be served except its own organised demands and impulses, will be very soon like the force of steam driving an engine without the driver or an engine in which the locomotive force has made the driver its servant and not its controller. It can only add the uncontrollable impetus of a high-crested or broad-based Titanism, or it may be even a nether flaming demonism, to the Nature-forces of the material world with the intellect as its servant, an impetus of measureless unresting creation, appropriation, expansion which will end in something violent, huge and colossal, foredoomed in its very nature to excess and ruin, because light is not in it nor the soul's truth nor the sanction of the gods and their calm eternal will and knowledge.

Beyond the vital subjectivism there is the possibility of a mental and psychic subjectivism. What would this greater subjectivism be able to achieve if it succeeds in exerting a powerful influence on the life of the individual and society?

This greater idea would realise that the elevation of the human existence will come not through material efficiency alone or the complex play of his vital and dynamic powers mastering through the aid of the intellect the energies of physical nature for the satisfaction of the life-instincts, which can only be an intensification of his present mode of existence, but through the greatness of his mental and psychic being and a discovery bringing forward an organisation of his vast subliminal nature and its forces. It would see in life an opportunity for the joy and power of knowledge, for the joy and power of beauty, for the joy and power of the human will mastering not only physical Nature, but vital and mental Nature. It might discover her secret yet undreamed of mind-powers and life-powers and use them for a freer liberation of man from the limitations of his shackled bodily life. It might arrive at new psychic relations, a more sovereign power of the idea to realise itself in the act, inner means of overcoming obstacles of distance and division which would cast into insignificance even the last miraculous achievements of material Science. A development of this kind is far enough away from the dreams of the mass of men, but there are certain pale hints and presages of such a possibility and ideas which lead to it are already held by a great number who are perhaps in this respect the yet unrecognised vanguard of humanity. It is not impossible that behind the confused morning voices of the hour a light of this kind, still below the horizon, may be waiting to ascend with its splendours.

Such a turn of human thought, effort, ideas of life, if it took hold of the communal mind, would evidently lead to a profound revolution throughout the whole range of human existence. It would give it from the first a new tone and atmosphere, a loftier spirit, wider horizons, a greater aim. It might easily develop a Science which would bring the powers of the physical world into a real and not only a contingent and mechanical subjection and open perhaps the doors of other worlds. It might develop an achievement of Art and Beauty which would make the greatness of the past a comparatively little thing and would save the world from the astonishingly callous reign of utilitarian ugliness that even now afflicts it. It would open up a closer and freer interchange between human minds and, it may well be hoped, a kindlier interchange between human hearts and lives. Nor need its achievements stop here, but might proceed to greater things of which these would be only the beginnings.

Would this mental and psychic subjectivism be free from the dangers that are found in the vital subjectivism?

This mental and psychic subjectivism would have its dangers, greater dangers even than those that attend a vitalistic subjectivism, because its powers of action also would be greater, but it would have what vitalistic subjectivism has not and cannot easily have, the chance of a detecting discernment, strong safeguards and a powerful liberating light. But still a subjective age of mankind must be an adventure full of perils and uncertainties as are all great adventures of the race. It may wander long before it finds itself or may not find itself at all and swing back to a new repetition of the cycle.

But is there also not this danger that the effort of mental and psychic subjectivism may succeed only with individuals but fail with the mass of humanity which even till the present day remains so firmly entrenched in its physical mentality? Is it conceivable that the average physical man can be rapidly uplifted to the mental and psychical heights and to the farther elevation of the Spirit?

This was one principal reason of the failure of past attempts to spiritualise mankind, that they endeavoured to spiritualise at once the material man by a sort of rapid miracle, and though that can be done, the miracle is not likely to be of an enduring character if it overleaps the stages of his ascent and leaves the intervening levels untrodden and therefore unmastered. The endeavour may succeed with individuals, — Indian thought would say with those who have made themselves ready in a past existence, — but it must fail with the mass. When it passes beyond the few, the forceful miracle of the Spirit flags; unable to transform by inner force, the new religion tries to save by machinery, is entangled in the mechanical turning of its own instruments, loses the spirit and perishes quickly or decays slowly. That is the fate which overtakes all attempts of the vitalistic, the intellectual and mental, the spiritual endeavour to deal with material man through his physical mind chiefly or alone; the endeavour is overpowered by the machinery it creates and becomes the slave and victim of the machine. That is the revenge which our material nature, herself mechanical, takes upon all such violent endeavours; she waits to master them by their concessions to her own law. If mankind is to be spiritualised, it must first in the mass cease to be the material or the vital man and become the psychic and the true mental being. It may be questioned whether such a mass progress or conversion is possible; but if it is not, then the spiritualisation of mankind as a whole is a chimera.

XXI

SUBJECTIVISM AND AND OBJECTIVISM (3)

What was the chief reason which turned the materialistic objectivism of the last century to subjectivism?

In Europe this materialistic objectivism has proceeded by the discovery of the laws of the physical universe and the economic and sociological conditions of human life as determined by the physical being of man, his environment, his evolutionary history, his physical and vital, his individual and collective need. But after a time it must become apparent that the knowledge of the physical world is not the whole of knowledge; it must appear that man is a mental as well as a physical and vital being and even much more essentially mental than physical or vital. Even though his psychology is strongly affected and limited by his physical being and environment, it is not at its roots determined by them, but constantly reacts, subtly determines their action, effects even their new-shaping by the force of his psychological demand on life. His economic state and social institutions are themselves governed by his psychological demand on the possibilities, circumstances, tendencies created by the relation between the mind and soul of humanity and its life and body. Therefore to find the truth of things and the law of his being in relation to that truth he must go deeper and fathom the subjective secret of himself and things as well as their objective forms and surroundings.

But could he not find this truth and this law by the power of his critical analytic intellect without having recourse to his deeper powers?

Not for very long. For in his study of himself and the world he cannot but come face to face with the soul in himself and the soul in the world and find it to be an entity so profound, so complex, so full of hidden secrets and powers that his intellectual reason betrays itself as an insufficient light and a fumbling seeker: it is successfully analytical only of superficialities and of what lies just behind the superficies. The need of a deeper knowledge must then turn him to the discovery of new powers and means within himself. He finds that he can only know himself entirely by becoming actively self-conscious and not merely self-critical, by more and more living in his soul and acting out of it rather than floundering on surfaces, by putting himself into conscious harmony with that which lies behind his superficial mentality and psychology and by enlightening his reason and making dynamic his action through this deeper light and power to which he thus opens. In this process the rationalistic ideal begins to subject itself to the ideal of intuitional knowledge and a deeper self-awareness; the utilitarian standard gives way to the aspiration towards self-consciousness and self-realisation; the rule of living according to the manifest laws of physical Nature is replaced by the effort towards living according to the veiled Law and Will and Power active in the life of the world and in the inner and outer life of humanity.

What changes did this new subjective Intuitionalism produce in the cultural activities of the modern age?

The art, music and literature of the world, always a sure index of the vital tendencies of the age, have undergone a profound revolution in the direction of an ever-deepening subjectivism. The great objective art and literature of the past no longer commands the mind of the new age. The first tendency was, as in thought so in literature, an increasing psychological vitalism which sought to represent penetratingly the most subtle psychological impulses and tendencies of man as they started to the surface in his emotional, aesthetic and vitalistic cravings and activities. Composed with great skill and subtlety but without any real insight into the law of man's being, these creations seldom got behind the reverse side of our surface emotions, sensations and actions which they minutely analysed in their details but without any wide or profound light of knowledge; they were perhaps more immediately interesting but ordinarily inferior as art to the old literature which at least seized firmly and with a large and powerful mastery on its province. Often they described the malady of Life rather than its health and power, or the riot and revolt of its cravings, vehement and therefore impotent and unsatisfied, rather than its dynamis of self-expression and self-possession. But to this movement which reached its highest creative power in Russia, there succeeded a turn towards a more truly psychological art, music and literature, mental, intuitional, psychic rather than vitalistic, departing in fact from a superficial vitalism as much as its predecessors departed from the objective mind of the past. This new movement largely aimed like the new philosophic Intuitionalism at a real rending of the veil, the seizure by the human mind of that which does not overtly express itself, the touch and penetration into the hidden soul of things. Much of it was still infirm, unsubstantial in its grasp on what it pursued, rudimentary in its forms, but it initiated a decisive departure of the human mind from its old moorings and pointed the direction in which it is being piloted on a momentous voyage of discovery, the discovery of a new world within which must eventually bring about the creation of a new world without in life and society. Art and literature seem definitely to have taken a turn towards a subjective search into what may be called the hidden inside of things and away from the rational and objective canon or nature.

In the field of education, as in the fields of art and literature, the subjective movement has brought about a definitive change in the ideals of the previous generation. What is the main consequence of this change?

Formerly, education was merely a mechanical forcing of the child's nature into arbitrary grooves of training and knowledge in which his individual subjectivity was the last thing considered, and his family upbringing was a constant repression and compulsory shaping of his habits, his thoughts, his character into the mould fixed for them by the conventional ideas or individual interests and ideals of the teachers and parents. The discovery that education must be a bringing out of the child's own intellectual and moral capacities to their highest possible value and must be based on the psychology of the child-nature was a step forward towards a more healthy because a more subjective system.

In what respect did this new discovery fall short of the complete truth about child-education? By what way could it arrive at this complete truth?

It fell short because it still regarded the child as an object to be handled and moulded by the teacher, to be educated. But at least there was a glimmering of the realisation that each human being is a self-developing soul and that the business of both parent and teacher is to enable and to help the child to educate himself, to develop his own intellectual, moral, aesthetic and practical capacities and to grow freely as an organic being, not to be kneaded and pressed into form like an inert plastic material. It is not yet realised what this soul is or that the true secret, whether with child or man, is to help him to find his deeper self, the real psychic entity within. That, if we ever give it a chance to come forward, and still more if we call it into the foreground as "the leader of the march set in our front", will itself take up most of the business of education out of our hands and develop the capacity of the psychological being towards a realisation of its potentialities of which our present mechanical view of life and man and external routine methods of dealing with them prevent us from having any experience or forming any conception. These new educational methods are on the straight way to this truer dealing. The closer touch attempted with the psychical entity behind the vital and physical mentality and an increasing reliance on its possibilities must lead to the ultimate discovery that man is inwardly a soul and a conscious power of the Divine and that the evocation of this real man within is the right object of education and indeed of all human life if it would find and live according to the hidden Truth and deepest law of its own being. That was the knowledge which the ancients sought to express through religious and social symbolism, and subjectivism is a road of return to the lost knowledge. First deepening man's inner experience, restoring perhaps on an unprecedented scale insight and self-knowledge to the race, it must end by revolutionising his social and collective self-expression.

XXII

SUBJECTIVISM AND OBJECTIVISM (4)

Modern psychology, which is still either completely under the influence of the objectivist view of life or only superficially subjective in some of its branches, considers all subjectivism, whose very principle is to turn within, as unhealthy introversion leading to morbidity and abnormality. The external reality is to its view the only safe province for human thought and action and so its advice is to be as extrovert and objective as possible. Is this not an evident exaggeration?

The materialistic thinker, erecting an opposition between the extrovert and the introvert, holds up the extrovert attitude for acceptance as the only safety: to go inward is to enter into darkness or emptiness or to lose the balance of the consciousness and become morbid; it is from outside that such inner life as one can construct is created, and its health is assured only by a strict reliance on its wholesome and nourishing outer sources, — the balance of the personal mind and life can only be secured by a firm support on external reality, for the material world is the sole fundamental reality. This may be true for the physical man, the born extrovert, who feels himself to be a creature of outward Nature; made by her and dependent on her, he would lose himself if he went inward: for him there is no inner being, no inner living. But the introvert of this distinction also has not the inner life; he is not a seer of the true inner self and of inner things, but the small mental man who looks superficially inside himself and sees there not his spiritual self but his life-ego, his mind-ego and becomes unhealthily preoccupied with the movements of this little pitiful dwarf creature. The idea or experience of an inner darkness when looking inwards is the first reaction of a mentality which has lived always on the surface and has no realised inner existence; it has only a constructed internal experience which depends on the outside world for the materials of its being. But to those into whose composition there has entered the power of a more inner living, the movement of going within and living within brings not a darkness or dull emptiness but an enlargement, a rush of new experience, a greater vision, a larger capacity, an extended life infinitely more real and various than the first pettiness of the life constructed for itself by our normal physical humanity, a joy of being which is larger and richer than any delight in existence that the outer vital man or the surface mental man can gain by their dynamic vital force and activity or subtlety and expansion of the mental existence. A silence, an entry into a wide or even immense or infinite emptiness is part of the inner spiritual experience; of this silence and void the physical mind has a certain fear, the small superficially active thinking or vital mind shrinks from it or dislikes it, — for it confuses the silence with mental and vital incapacity and the void with cessation or non-existence: but this silence is the silence of the Spirit which is the condition of a greater knowledge, power and bliss, and this emptiness is the emptying of the cup of our natural being, a liberation of it from its turbid contents so that it may be filled with the wine of God; it is the passage not into non-existence but to a greater existence. Even when the being turns towards cessation, it is a cessation not in non-existence but into some vast ineffable of spiritual being or the plunge into the incommunicable superconscience of the Absolute.

Bertrand Russell in his book The Conquest of Happiness *says: "We are all prone to the malady of the introvert, who with the manifold spectacle of the world spread out before him, turns away and gazes upon the emptiness within." Is this not a completely misleading statement?*

The word "introvert" has come into existence only recently and sounds like a companion of "pervert". Literally, it means one who is turned inwards. The Upanishad speaks of the doors of the senses that are turned outwards absorbing man in external things ("for their own sakes", I suppose?) and of the rare man among a million who turns his vision inwards and sees the self. Is that man an introvert? And is Russell's ideal man "interested in externals for their own sakes" — a Ramaswami the chef or Joseph the chauffeur, for instance — *homo externalis Russellius*, an extrovert? Or is an introvert one who has an inner life stronger than his external one, — the poet, the musician, the artist? Was Beethoven in his deafness bringing out music from within him an introvert? Or does it mean one who measures external things by an inner standard and is interested in them not "for their own sakes" but for their value to the soul's self-development, its psychic, religious, ethical or other self-expression? Are Tolstoy and Gandhi examples of introverts? or in another field — Goethe? or does it mean one who cares for external things only as they touch his own mind or else concern his own ego? But that would include 999,999 men out of every million.

What are external things? Russell is a mathematician. Are mathematical formulae external things even though they exist here only in the World-mind and the mind of Man? If not, is Russell, as mathematician, an introvert? Again, Yajnavalkya says that one loves the wife not for the sake of the wife, but for the self's sake, and so with other objects of interest or desire — whether the self be the inner self or the ego. In Yoga it is the valuing of external things in the terms of the desire of the ego that is discouraged — their only value is their value in the manifestation of the Divine. Who desires external things "for their own sakes" and not for some value to the conscious being? Even Cheloo, the day-labourer, is not interested in a two-anna piece for its own sake, but for some vital satisfaction it can bring him; even with the hoarding miser it is the same — it is his vital being's passion for possession that he satisfies and that is something not external but internal, part of his inner make-up, the unseen personality that moves inside behind the veil of the body.

Why is it so difficult for the materialist thinker to concede substantial reality to the subjective and supraphysical order of existence?

The objective and the physical order or reality is convincing to the physical or externalising mind because it is directly obvious to the senses, while of the subjective and the supraphysical that mind has no means of knowledge except from fragmentary signs and data and inferences which are at every step liable to error. Our subjective movements and inner experiences are a domain of happenings as real as any outward physical happenings; but if the individual mind can know something of its own phenomena by direct experience, it is ignorant of what happens in the consciousness of others except by analogy with its own or such signs, data, inferences as its outward observation can give it. I am therefore inwardly real to myself, but the invisible life of others has only an indirect reality to me except in so far as it impinges on my own mind, life and senses. This is the limitation of the physical mind of man, and it creates in him a habit of believing entirely only in the physical and of doubting or challenging all that does not come into accord with his own experience or his own scope of understanding or square with his own standard or sum of established knowledge.

In recent times this attitude of the common physical mind has been raised into a valid standard of knowledge. It has been held that all truth must be referred to the judgment of the personal mind of every man or else it must be verifiable by a common experience in order to be valid. Is not this standard quite inadequate and even false?

Obviously this is a false standard of reality and of knowledge, since this means the sovereignty of the normal or average mind and its limited capacity and experience, the exclusion of what is supernormal or beyond the average intelligence. In its extreme, this claim of the individual to be the judge of everything is an egoistic illusion, a superstition of the physical mind, in the mass a gross and vulgar error. The truth behind it is that each man has to think for himself, know for himself according to his capacity, but his judgment can be valid only on condition that he is ready to learn and open always to a larger knowledge. It is reasoned that to depart from the physical standard and the principle of personal or universal verification will lead to gross delusions and the admission of unverified truth and subjective phantasy into the realm of knowledge. But error and delusion and the introduction of personality and one's own subjectivity into the pursuit of knowledge are always present, and the physical or objective standards and methods do not exclude them. The probability of error is no reason for refusing to attempt discovery, and subjective discovery must be pursued by a subjective method of enquiry, observation and verification; research into the supraphysical must evolve, accept and test an appropriate means and methods other than those by which one examines the constituents of physical objects and the processes of Energy in material Nature.

To refuse to enquire upon any general ground preconceived and *a priori* is an obscurantism as prejudicial to the extension of knowledge as the religious obscurantism which opposed in Europe the extension of scientific discovery. The greatest inner discoveries, the experience of self-being, the cosmic consciousness, the inner calm of the liberated spirit, the direct effect of mind upon mind, the knowledge of things by consciousness in direct contact with other consciousness or with its objects, most spiritual experiences of any value, cannot be brought before the tribunal of the common mentality which has no experience of these things and takes its own absence or incapacity of experience as a proof of their invalidity or their non-existence. Physical truth of formulas, generalisations, discoveries founded upon physical observation can be so referred, but even there a training of capacity is needed before one can truly understand and judge; it is not every untrained mind that can follow the mathematics of relativity or other difficult scientific truths or judge the validity either of their result or their process. All reality, all experience must indeed, to be held as true, be capable of verification by a same or similar experience; so, in fact, all men can have a spiritual experience and can follow it out and verify it in themselves, but only when they have acquired the capacity or can follow the inner methods by which that experience and verification are made possible. It is necessary to dwell on these obvious and elementary truths because the opposite ideas have been sovereign in a recent period of human mentality, — they are now only receding, — and have stood in the way of the development of a vast domain of possible knowledge. It is of supreme importance for the human spirit to be free to sound the depths of inner or subliminal reality, of spiritual and of what is still superconscient reality, and not to immure itself in the physical mind and its narrow domain of objective external solidities; for in that way alone can there come liberation from the Ignorance in which our mentality dwells and a release into a complete consciousness, a true and integral self-realisation and self-knowledge.

XXIII

SUBJECTIVISM AND OBJECTIVISM (5)

As the objectivist view of the materialistic thinker denies substantial reality to our subjective existence, so the subjectivist view of a certain school of Idealistic thought refuses to concede independent reality to all objective existence. According to this school, all that exists is a subjective creation of mind, a structure of consciousness, and the idea of an objective reality independent of consciousness is an illusion, since we can have no evidence of any such independent self-existence of things. How far is this view tenable?

It is clear that a Mind of the nature of our surface intelligence can be only a secondary power of existence. For it bears the stamp of incapacity and ignorance as a sign that it is derivative and not the original creatrix; we see that it does not know or understand the objects it perceives, it has no automatic control of them; it has to acquire a laboriously built knowledge and controlling power. This initial incapacity could not be there if these objects were the Mind's own structures, creations of its self-Power.

But if we suppose a universal Mind of the same character as our mind, could not that well be the creator of the universe?

The nature of Mind as we know it is an Ignorance seeking for knowledge; it is a knower of fractions and worker of divisions striving to arrive at a sum, to piece together a whole, — it is not possessed of the essence of things or their totality: a universal Mind of the same character might know the sum of its divisions by force of its universality, but it would still lack the essential knowledge, and without the essential knowledge there could be no true integral knowledge.

An infinite Mind constituted in the terms of mentality as we know it might possibly construct an accidental cosmos of conflicting possibilities and it might shape it into something shifting, something always transient, something ever uncertain in its drift, neither real nor unreal, possessed of no definite end or aim but only an endless succession of momentary aims leading, — since there is no superior directing power of knowledge — eventually nowhither. Nihilism or Illusionism or some kindred philosophy is the only logical conclusion of such a pure noumenalism. The cosmos so constructed would be a presentation or reflection of something not itself, but always and to the end a false presentation, a distorted reflection; all cosmic existence would be a Mind struggling to work out fully its imaginations, but not succeeding, because they have no imperative basis of self-truth; overpowered and carried forward by the stream of its own past energies, it would be borne onward indeterminately forever without issue unless or until it can either slay itself or fall into an eternal stillness. That traced to its roots is Nihilism and Illusionism and it is the only wisdom if we suppose that our human mentality or anything at all like it represents the highest cosmic force and the original conception at work in the universe.

Would this be true even of an infinite Mind free from the limitations of our mind? Could not such a Mind, infinite, omniscient and omnipotent, be the original creator of the universe?

But such a Mind would be something quite different from the definition of mind as we know it: it would be something beyond mentality; it would be the supramental Truth. An infinite, omniscient, omnipotent Mind would not be mind at all but supramental knowledge. Mind, as we know it, is not the original constructor of the universe: it is an intermediary power valid for certain actualities of being; an agent, an intermediary, it actualises possibilities and has its share in the creation, but the real creatrix is a Consciousness, an Energy inherent in the transcendent and cosmic Spirit.

We have then to admit that the subjectivist view of reality by itself does not represent the complete truth and the objectivist view has also an element of truth in it?

It is true that there is no such thing as an objective reality independent of consciousness; but at the same time there is a truth in objectivity and it is this, that the reality of things resides in something that is within them and is independent of the interpretation our mind gives to them and of the structures it builds upon its observation. These structures constitute the mind's subjective image or figure of the universe, but the universe and its objects are not a mere image or figure. They are in essence creations of consciousness, but of a consciousness that is one with being, whose substance is the substance of Being and whose creations too are of that substance, therefore real. In this view the world cannot be a purely subjective creation of Consciousness; the subjective and the objective truth of things are both real, they are two sides of the same Reality.

XXIV

MATERIALISM (1)

Materialism, from which the objectivist theory of reality and knowledge was derived and which has now lost much of the ground it held in the last century, has been credited with the creation of a large number of great evils and its decline and passing away has been proclaimed, especially by the idealists and the religionists, as a fortunate deliverance for the human spirit. Is this accusation wholly valid? Has materialism been a force only for the retardation of knowledge and deviation from the true path of progress?

All that materialism is accused of may have and much of it has its truth. But most things that the human mind thus alternately trumpets and bans are a double skein. They come to us with opposite faces, their good side and their bad, a dark aspect of error and a bright of truth; and it is as we look upon one or the other visage that we swing to our extremes of opinion or else oscillate between them.

We have then to admit that the materialism of the previous age, in spite of its basic limitations, did contribute something to the positive advancement of human knowledge and civilisational progress?

This age of which materialism was the portentous offspring and in which it had figured first as petulant rebel and aggressive thinker, then as a grave and strenuous preceptor of mankind, has been by no means a period of mere error, calamity and degeneration, but rather a most powerful creative epoch of humanity. Examine impartially its results. Not only has it immensely widened and filled in the knowledge of the race and accustomed it to a great patience of research, scrupulosity, accuracy, — if it has done that only in one large sphere of inquiry, it has still prepared for the extension of the same curiosity, intellectual rectitude, power for knowledge to other and higher fields, — not only has it with an unexampled force and richness of invention brought and put into our hands, for much evil, but also for much good, discoveries, instruments, practical powers, conquests, conveniences which, however we may declare their insufficiency for our highest interests, yet few of us would care to relinquish, but it has also, paradoxical as that might at first seem, strengthened man's idealism. On the whole, it has given him a kindlier hope and humanised his nature. Tolerance is greater, liberty has increased, charity is more a matter of course, peace, if not yet practicable, is growing at least imaginable. Latterly the thought of the eighteenth century which promulgated secularism has been much scouted and belittled, that of the nineteenth which developed it, riddled with adverse criticism and overpassed. Still they worshipped no mean godheads. Reason, science, progress, freedom, humanity were their ideals, and which of these idols, if idols they are, would we like or ought we, if we are wise, to cast down into the mire or leave as poor unworshipped relics on the wayside? If there are other and yet greater godheads or if the visible forms adored were only clay or stone images or the rites void of the inmost knowledge, yet has their cult been for us a preliminary initiation and the long material sacrifice prepared us for a greater religion.

Science and reason which were the two principal powers by which the entire structure of materialistic thought was built are also now discredited along with materialism especially as they fostered scepticism, agnosticism and atheism. But have we not to concede that they too had their utility, even a sort of a necessity in the progressive development of human knowledge?

Reason is not the supreme light, but yet it is always a necessary light-bringer and until it has been given its rights and allowed to judge and purify our first infrarational instincts, impulses, rash fervours, crude beliefs, and blind prejudgments, we are not altogether ready for the full unveiling of a greater inner luminary. Science is a right knowledge, in the end only of processes, but still the knowledge of processes too is part of a total wisdom and essential to a wide and a clear approach towards deeper Truth behind. If it has laboured mainly in the physical field, if it has limited itself and bordered or overshadowed its light with a certain cloud of wilful ignorance, still one had to begin this method somewhere and the physical field is the first, the nearest, the easiest for the kind and manner of inquiry undertaken. Ignorance of one side of Truth or the choice of a partial ignorance or ignoring for better concentration on another side is often a necessity of our imperfect mental nature. It is unfortunate if ignorance becomes dogmatic and denies what it has refused to examine, but still no permanent harm need have been done if this willed self-limitation is compelled to disappear when the occasion of its utility is exhausted. Now that we have founded rigorously our knowledge of the physical, we can go forward with a much firmer step to a more open, secure and luminous repossession of mental and psychic knowledge. Even spiritual truths are likely to gain from it, not a loftier or more penetrating, — that is with difficulty possible, — but an ampler light and fuller self-expression.

> *Critics of materialism attach no substantial value to the help it rendered to human progress and advancement of freedom and humanitarianism because all this progress and advancement was confined to man's outer life while true progress, freedom and charity, in their view, could only be found in man's inner being. Is this criticism entirely justified?*

Progress is the very heart of the significance of human life, for it means our evolution into greater and richer being; and the materialistic ages by insisting on it, by forcing us to recognise it as our aim and our necessity, by making impossible hereafter the attempt to subsist in the dullness or the gross beatitude of a stationary self-content, have done a priceless service to the earth-life and cleared the ways of heaven. Outward progress was the greater part of its aim and the inward is the more essential, but the inward too is not complete if the outward is left out of account. Even if the insistence of our progress falls for a time too exclusively on growth in one field, still all movement forward is helpful and must end by giving a greater force and a larger meaning to our need of growth in deeper and higher provinces of our being. Freedom is a godhead whose greatness only the narrowly limited mind, the State-worshipper or the crank of reaction can now deny. No doubt, again, the essential is an inner freedom; but if without the inner realisation the outer attempt at liberty may prove at last a vain thing, yet to pursue an inner liberty and perpetuate an outer slavery or to rejoice in an isolated release and leave mankind to its chains was also an anomaly that had to be exploded, a confined and too self-centred ideal. Humanity is not the highest godhead; God is more than humanity; but in humanity too we have to find and to serve Him. The cult of humanity means an increasing kindliness, tolerance, charity, helpfulness, solidarity, universality, unity, fullness of individual and collective growth, and towards these things we are advancing much more rapidly than was possible in any previous age, if still with sadly stumbling footsteps and some fierce relapses. The cult of our other human selves within the cult of the Divine comes closer to us as our large ideal. To have brought even one of these things a step nearer, to have helped to settle them with whatever imperfect expression and formula in our minds, to have accelerated our movement towards them are strong achievements, noble services.

> *But it is contended that these great movements were not the results of materialism because the urge towards them had been long active in the mind of the race and the seeds from which they naturally grew had been sown a long time back. The principle of humanitarianism, for example, was first made prominent by Christianity and Buddhism which preached insistently compassion and love. Materialism*

therefore cannot be credited with originating these high ideals which existed in previous religious cultures though it gave them a fuller development. Is this view quite true?

This is the truth, but not the whole truth. The old religious cultures were often admirable in the ensemble and always in some of their parts, but if they had not been defective, they could neither have been so easily breached, nor would there have been the need of a secularist age to bring out the results the religions had sown.

What were the defects in these old religious cultures which prevented the full realisation of the social ideals of progress, freedom and liberalism?

Their faults were those of a certain narrowness and exclusive vision. Concentrated, intense in their ideal and intensive in their effect, their expansive influence on the human mind was small. They isolated too much their action in the individual, limited too narrowly the working of their ideals in the social order, tolerated for instance, and even utilised for the ends of Church and creed, an immense amount of cruelty and barbarism which were contrary to the spirit and truth from which they had started. What they discouraged in the soul of the individual, they yet maintained in the action and the frame of society, seemed hardly to conceive of a human order delivered from these blots. The depth and fervour of their aspiration had for its shadow a want of intellectual clarity, an obscurity which confused their working and baulked the expansion of their spiritual elements. They nourished too a core of asceticism and hardly cared to believe in the definite amelioration of the earth-life, despised by them as a downfall or a dolorous descent or imperfection of the human spirit, or whatever earthly hope they admitted, saw itself postponed to the millennial end of things. A belief in the vanity of human life or of existence itself suited better the preoccupation with an aim beyond earth. Perfection, ethical growth, liberation became individual ideals and figured too much as an isolated preparation of the soul for the beyond. The social effect of the religious temperament, however potentially considerable, was cramped by excessive other-worldliness and distrust in the intellect accentuated to obscurantism.

But did not materialism which prevailed in the secularist centuries that followed these old religious cultures go very much to the opposite extreme?

The secularist centuries weighed the balance down very much in the opposite direction. They turned the mind of the race wholly earthwards and manwards, but by insisting on intellectual clarity, reason, justice, freedom, tolerance, humanity, by putting these forward and putting the progress of the race and its perfectibility as an immediate rule for the earthly life to be constantly pressed towards and not shunting off the social ideal to doomsday to be miraculously effected by some last divine intervention and judgment, they cleared the way for a collective advance. For they made these nobler possibilities of mankind more imperative to the practical intelligence. If they lost sight of heaven or missed the spiritual sense of the ideals they took over from earlier ages, yet by this rational and practical insistence on them they drove them home to the thinking mind. Even their too mechanical turn developed from a legitimate desire to find some means for making the effective working of these ideals a condition of the very structure of society. Materialism was only the extreme intellectual result of this earthward and human turn of the race mind.

What was the intention of the Time-spirit in turning the mind of the race so exclusively to materialistic pursuits and to the intensive exploration and mastery of physical Nature?

It was an intellectual machinery used by the Time-spirit to secure for a good space the firm fixing of that exclusive turn of thought and endeavour, a strong rivet of opinion to hold the mind of man to it for as long as it might be needed. Man does need to develop firmly in all his earthly parts, to fortify and perfect his body, his life, his outward-going mind, to take full possession of the earth, his dwelling-place, to know and utilise physical Nature, enrich his environment and satisfy by the aid of a generalised intelligence his evolving mental, vital and physical being. That is not all his need, but it is a great and initial part of it and of human perfection. Its full meaning appears afterwards; for only in the beginning an impulse of his life appears, in the end and really it will be seen to have been a need of his soul, a preparing of fit instruments and the creating of a fit environment for a diviner life. He has been set here to serve God's ways upon earth and fulfil the Godhead in man and he must not despise earth or reject the basis given for the first powers and potentialities of the Godhead. When his thought and aim have persisted too far in that direction, he need not complain if he is swung back for a time towards the other extreme, to a negative or a positive, a covert or an open materialism. It is Nature's violent way of setting right her own excess in him.

XXV

MATERIALISM (2)

Why did materialism become so powerful a force in the last century? Was its influence derived from some basic universal truth to which it gave a distinctive formulation?

The intellectual force of materialism comes from its response to a universal truth of existence. Our dominant opinions have always two forces behind them, a need of our nature and a truth of universal existence from which the need arises. We have the material and vital need because life in Matter is our actual basis, the earthward turn of our minds because earth is and was intended to be the foundation here for the workings of the Spirit. When indeed we scan with a scrupulous intelligence the face that universal existence presents to us or study where we are one with it or what in it all seems most universal and permanent, the first answer we get is not spiritual but material. The seers of the Upanishads saw this with their penetrating vision and when they gave this expression of our first apparently complete, eventually insufficient view of Being, "Matter is the Brahman, from Matter all things are born, by Matter they exist, to Matter they return," they fixed the formula of universal truth of which all materialistic thought and physical science are a recognition, an investigation, a filling in of its significant details, elucidations, justifying phenomena and revelatory processes, the large universal comment of Nature upon a single text.

But since the truth of Matter is only the first fact of our normal experience and not the complete or final truth, why was it taken to be the sole truth of existence to the exclusion of all other higher universal truths?

Matter surely is here our basis, the one thing that is and persists, while life, mind, soul and all else appear in it as a secondary phenomenon, seem somehow to arise out of it, subsist by feeding upon it, — therefore the word used in the Upanishads for Matter is *annam,* food, — and disappear from our viewpoint. Apparently the existence of Matter is necessary to them, their existence does not appear to be one whit necessary to Matter. The Being does present himself at first with this face, inexorably, as if claiming to be that and nothing else, insisting that his material base and its need shall first be satisfied and, until that is done, grimly persistent with little or with no regard for our idealistic susceptibilities and caring nothing if he breaks through the delicate net of our moral, our aesthetic and our other finer perceptions. They have the hope of their reign, but meanwhile this is the first visage of universal existence and we have not to hide our face from it any more than could Arjuna from the terrible figure of the Divine on the battlefield of Kurukshetra, or attempt to escape and evade it as Shiva, when there rose around him the many stupendous forms of the original Energy, fled from the vision of it to this and that quarter, forgetful of his own godhead. We must look existence in the face in whatever aspect it confronts us and be strong to find within as well as behind it the Divine.

But why should science which impartially seeks for the complete truth of phenomena rule out from its enquiry all the evidence of the greater and independent truths of our biological, psychological and spiritual existence or explain them away as merely secondary powers dependent on the primary and the fundamental reality of Matter?

Physical science must necessarily to its own first view be materialistic, because so long as it deals with the physical, it has for its own truth's sake to be physical both in its standpoint and method; it must interpret the material universe first in the language of the material Brahman, because these are its primary and its general terms and all others come second, subsequently, are a special syllabary. To follow a self-indulgent course from the beginning would lead at once towards fancies and falsities.

Initially, science is justified in resenting any call on it to indulge in another kind of imagination and intuition. Anything that draws it out of the circle of the phenomena of objects, as they are represented to the senses and their instrumental prolonga-tions, and away from the dealings of the reason with them by a rigorous testing of experience and experimentation, must distract it from its task and is inadmissible. It cannot allow the bringing in of the human view of things; it has to interpret man in the terms of the cosmos, not the cosmos in the terms of man. The too facile conclusion of the idealist that since things only exist as known to consciousness, they can exist only by consciousness and must be creations of the mind, has no meaning for it; it first has to inquire what consciousness is, whether it is not a result rather than a cause of Matter, coming into being, as it seems to do, only in the frame of a material inconscient universe and apparently able to exist only on the condition that that has been previously established. Starting from Matter, science has to be at least hypothetically materialistic.

But though this may be an initial necessity for science for firmly establishing the truth of Matter, must it not, after that necessity is over, break through the narrow shackles of the materialistic theory and widen out its inquiry into the greater realms of Life, Mind and Spirit?

When the action of the material principle, the first to organise itself, has been to some extent well understood, then can this science go on to consider what claim to be quite other terms of our being, — life and mind. But first it is forced to ask itself whether both mind and life are not, as they seem to be, special consequences of the material evolution, themselves powers and movements of Matter. After and if this explanation has failed to cover and to elucidate the facts, it can be more freely investigated whether they are not quite other principles of being. Many philosophical questions arise, as, whether they have entered into Matter and whence or were always in it, and if so, whether they are for ever less and subordinate in action or are in their essential power greater, whether they are contained in it only or really contain it, whether they are subsequent and dependent on its previous appearance or only that in their apparent organisation here but in real being and power anterior to it and Matter itself dependent on the essential pre-existence of life and mind. A greater question comes, whether mind itself is the last term or there is something beyond, whether soul is only an apparent result and phenomenon of the interaction of mind, life and body or we have here an independent term of our being and of all being, greater, anterior, ultimate, all Matter containing and contained in a secret spiritual consciousness, spirit the first, last and eternal, the Alpha and the Omega, the OM. For experiential philosophy either Matter, Mind, Life or Spirit may be the Being but none of these higher principles can be made securely the basis of our thought against all intellectual questioning until the materialistic hypothesis has first been given a chance and tested. That may in the end turn out to have been the use of the materialistic investigation of the universe and its inquiry the greatest possible service to the finality of the spiritual explanation of the universe.

What are the gates of escape by which materialistic knowledge can get away from its self-imprisoning limitations?

Physical science has before its eye two eternal factors of existence, Matter and Energy, and no others at all are needed in the account of its operations. Mind dealing with the facts and relations of Matter and Energy as they are arranged to the senses in experience and continuative experiment and are analysed by the reason, would be a sufficient definition of physical science. Its first regard is on Matter as the one principle of being and on energy only as phenomenon of Matter, but in the end one questions whether it is not the other way round, all things the action of Energy and Matter only the field, body and instrument of her workings. The first view is quantitative and purely mechanical, the second lets in a qualitative and a more spiritual element. We do not at once leap out of the materialistic circle, but we see an opening in it which may widen into an outlet when, stirred by this suggestion, we look at life and mind not merely as a phenomenon in Matter, but as energies, and see that they are other energies than the material with their own peculiar qualities, powers and workings. If indeed all action of life and mind could be reduced, as it was once hoped, to none but material quantitative and mechanical, to mathematical, physiological and chemical terms, the opening would cease to be an outlet; it would be chocked. That attempt has failed and there is no sign of its ever being successful. Only a limited range of the phenomena of life and mind could be satisfied by a purely bio-physical, psycho-physical or bio-psychical explanation, and even if more could be dealt with by these data, still they would only have been accounted for on one side of their mystery, the lower end. Life and Mind, like the Vedic Agni, have their two extremities hidden in a secrecy, and we should by this way only have hold of the tail end, the head would still be mystic and secret. To know more we must have studied not only the actual or possible action of body and Matter on mind and life, but explored all the possible action of mind too on body and life; that opens undreamed vistas. And there is always the vast field of the action of mind in itself and on itself, which needs for its elucidation another, a mental, a psychic science.

Having examined and explained Matter by physical methods and in the language of the material Brahman, — it is not really explained, but let that pass, — having failed to carry that way of knowledge into other fields beyond a narrow limit, we must then at least consent to scrutinise life and mind by methods appropriate to them and explain their facts in the language and tokens of the vital and mental Brahman. We may discover then where and how these tongues of the one existence render the same truth and throw light on each other's phrases, and discover too perhaps another, high, brilliant and revealing speech which may shine out as the definitive all-explaining word. That can only be if we pursue these other sciences too in the same spirit as the physical, with a scrutiny not only of their obvious and first actual phenomena, but of all the countless untested potentialities of mental and psychic energy, and with a free unlimited experimentation. We shall find out that their ranges of the unknown are immense. We shall perceive that until the possibilities of mind and spirit are better explored and their truths better known, we cannot yet pronounce the last all-ensphering formula of universal existence. Very early in this process the materialistic circle will be seen opening up on all its sides until it rapidly breaks up and disappears. Adhering still to the essential rigorous method of science, though not to its purely physical instrumentation, scrutinising, experimenting, holding nothing as established which cannot be scrupulously and universally verified, we shall still arrive at supraphysical certitudes. There are other means, there are greater approaches, but this line of access too can lead to the one universal Truth.

What will remain as the lasting contribution of the materialistic thought when the progressive mind of humanity has passed beyond it into higher truths of existence?

Three things will remain from the labour of the secularist centuries; truth of the physical world and its importance, the scientific method of knowledge, — which is to induce nature and Being to reveal their own way of being and proceeding, not hastening to put upon them our own impositions of idea and imagination, *adhyāropa*, — and last, though very far from least, the truth and importance of the earth life and the human endeavour, its evolutionary meaning. They will remain, but will turn to another sense and disclose greater issues. Surer of our hope and our labour, we shall see them all transformed into the light of a vaster and more intimate world-knowledge and self-knowledge.

Second Series

I

ART FOR ART'S SAKE

The slogan "Art for Art's sake" was very popular at one time though now its popularity seems to be on the decline. What is the real issue behind this slogan?

But what, after all, is meant by this slogan? Is it meant, as I think it was when the slogan first came into use, that the technique, the artistry is all in all? The contention would then be that it does not matter what you write or paint or sculpt or what music you make or about what you make it so long as it is beautiful writing, competent painting, good sculpture, fine music. It is very evidently true in a certain sense, — in this sense that whatever is perfectly expressed or represented or interpreted under the conditions of a given art proves itself by that very fact to be legitimate material for the artist's labour. But that free admission cannot be confined only to all objects, however common or deemed to be vulgar, — an apple, a kitchen pail, a donkey, a dish of carrots, — it can give a right of citizenship in the domain of art to a moral theme or thesis, a philosophic conclusion, a social experiment; even the Five Years' Plan or the proceedings of a District Board or the success of a drainage scheme, an electric factory or a big hotel can be brought, after the most modern or the still more robustious Bolshevik mode, into the artist's province. For, technique being all, the sole question would be whether he as poet, novelist, dramatist, painter or sculptor has been able to triumph over the difficulties and bring out creatively the possibilities of his subject. There is no logical basis here for accepting an apple and rejecting the Apple-Cart. But still you may say that at least the object of the artist must be art only, — even if he treats ethical, social or political questions, he must not make it his main object to wing with the enthusiasm of aesthetic creation a moral, social or political aim. But if in doing it he satisfies the conditions of his art, shows a perfect technique and in it beauty, power, perfection, why not? The moralist, preacher, philosopher, social or political enthusiast is often doubled with an artist — as shining proofs and examples there are Plato and Shelley, to go no farther. Only, you can say of him on the basis of this theory that as a work of art his creation should be judged by its success of craftsmanship and not by its contents; it is not made greater by the value of his ethical ideas, his enthusiasms or his metaphysical seekings.

But how far is this theory true? Is technique all in all in Art and substance of no importance?

The theory itself is true only up to a certain point. For technique is a means of expression; one does not write merely to use beautiful words or paint for the sole sake of line and colour, there is something that one is trying through these means to express or to discover.

What is that something?

The first answer would be — it is the creation, it is the discovery of Beauty. Art is for that alone and can be judged only by its revelation or discovery of Beauty. Whatever is capable of being manifested as Beauty is the material of the artist. But there is not only physical beauty in the world — there is moral, intellectual, spiritual beauty also. Still, one might say that "Art for Art's sake" means that only what is aesthetically beautiful must be expressed and all that contradicts the aesthetic sense of beauty must be avoided. Art has nothing to do with Life in itself, things in themselves, Good, Truth or the Divine for their own sake, but only in so far as they appeal to some aesthetic sense of beauty, — and that would seem to be a sound basis for excluding the Five Years' Plan, a moral sermon or a philosophical treatise.

But is it not a fact that beauty is something which is not in the object itself but in the consciousness that perceives it?

Art for Art's Sake

We know that an artist can perceive beauty in things that seem plain and ugly and even repellent to others.

There is a certain state of Yogic consciousness in which all things become beautiful to the eye of the seer, simply because they spiritually are — because they are a rendering in line and form of the quality and force of existence, of the consciousness, of the Ananda that rules the worlds, — of the hidden Divine. What a thing is to the exterior sense may not be, often is not beautiful for the ordinary aesthetic vision, but the Yogin sees in it the something More which the external eye does not see, he sees the soul behind, the self and spirit, he sees too lines, hues, harmonies and expressive dispositions which are not to the first surface sight visible or seizable. It may be said that he brings into the object something that is in himself, transmutes it by abiding out of his own being to it — as the artist too does something of the same kind but in another way. It is not quite that however; what the Yogin sees, what the artist sees, is there, his is a transmuting vision because it is a revealing vision; he discovers behind what the object appears to be, the something More that it is. And so from this point of view of a realised supreme harmony all is or can be subject matter for the artist, because in all he can discover and reveal the Beauty that is everywhere. Again, we land ourselves in a devastating catholicity; for here too one cannot pull up short at any given line. It may be a hard saying that one must or may discover and reveal beauty in a pig or its poke or in a parish pump or an advertisement of somebody's pills, and yet something like that seems to be what modern Art and Literature are trying with vigour and conscientious labour to do. By extension one ought to be able to extract beauty equally well out of morality or social reform or a political caucus or allow at least that all these things can, if he wills, become legitimate subjects for the artist. Here, too, one cannot say that it is on condition he thinks of beauty only and does not make moralising or social reform or a political idea his main object. For if with that idea foremost in his mind he still produces a great work of art, discovering Beauty as he moves to his aim, proving himself, in spite of his unaesthetic preoccupations, a great artist, it is all we can justly ask from him, whatever his starting-point, to be a creator of Beauty. Art is discovery and revelation of Beauty, and we can say nothing more by way of prohibitive or limiting rule.

Is there then no difference between this view of Art and the Yogin's vision of universal beauty?

There is one thing more that can be said, and that makes a big difference. In the Yogin's vision of universal beauty, all becomes beautiful, but all is not reduced to a single level. There are gradations, there is a hierarchy in this All-Beauty and we see that it depends on the ascending power (Vibhuti) of Consciousness and Ananda that expresses itself in the object. All is the Divine, but some things are more divine than others. In the artist's vision too there are or can be gradations, a hierarchy of values. Shakespeare can get dramatic and therefore aesthetic values out of Dogberry and Malvolio and he is as thorough a creative artist in his treatment of them as in his handling of Macbeth or Lear. But if we had only Dogberry or Malvolio to testify to Shakespeare's genius, no Macbeth, no Lear, would he be so great a dramatic artist and creator as he now is? It is in the varying possibilities of one subject or another that there lies an immense difference. Apelles' grapes deceived the birds that came to peck at them, but there was more aesthetic content in the Zeus of Pheidias, a greater content of consciousness and therefore of Ananda to express and with it to fill in and intensify the essential principle of Beauty, even though the essence of beauty may be realised perhaps with equal aesthetic perfection by either artist and in either theme.

Does this mean that for a complete creation of Art something more than the discovery of beauty is required?

Just as technique is not all, so even Beauty is not all in Art. Art is not only technique or form of Beauty, not only the discovery or the expression of Beauty — it is a self-expression of Consciousness under the conditions of aesthetic vision and a perfect execution. Or, to put it otherwise, there are not only aesthetic values, but life-values, mind-values, soul-values that enter into Art. The artist puts out into form not only the powers of his own consciousness, but the powers of the Consciousness that has made the worlds and their objects. And if that Consciousness according to the Vedantic view is fundamentally equal everywhere, it is still in manifestation not an equal power in all things. There is more of the Divine expression in the Vibhuti than in the common man, *prākṛto janaḥ;* in some forms of life there are less potentialities for the self-expression of the Spirit than in others. And there are also gradations of consciousness which make a difference, if not in the aesthetic value or greatness of a work of art, yet in its contents-value. Homer makes beauty out of man's outward life and action and stops there. Shakespeare rises one step further and reveals to us a life-soul and life-forces and life-values to which Homer had no access. In Valmiki and Vyasa there is the constant presence of great Idea-Forces and Ideals supporting life and its movements which were beyond the scope of Homer and Shakespeare. And beyond the Ideals and Idea-Forces even there are other presences, more inner or inmost realities, a soul behind things and beings, the spirit and its powers, which could be the subject matter of an art still more rich and deep and abundant in its interest than any of these could be. A poet finding these and giving them a voice with a genius equal to that of the poets of the past might not be greater than they in a purely aesthetic valuation, but his art's contents-value, its consciousness-values could be deeper and higher and much fuller than in any achievement before him. There is something here that goes beyond any consideration of Art for Art's sake or Art for Beauty's sake; for while these stress usefully sometimes the indispensable first elements of artistic creation, they would limit too much the creation itself if they stood for the exclusion of the something More that compels Art to change always in its constant seeking for more and more that must be expressed of the concealed or the revealed Divine, of the individual and the universal or the transcendent Spirit.

What are the elements constituting perfect Art? What should be the full aim of our aesthetic endeavour?

If we take these three elements as making the whole of Art, perfection of expressive form, discovery of beauty, revelation of the soul and essence of things and the powers of creative consciousness and Ananda of which they are the vehicles, then we shall get perhaps a solution which includes the two sides of the controversy and reconciles their difference. Art for Art's sake certainly; Art as a perfect form and discovery of Beauty; but also Art for the soul's sake, the spirit's sake and the expression of all that the soul, the spirit wants to seize through the medium of beauty. In that self-expression there are grades and hierarchies, widenings and steps that lead to the summits. And not only to enlarge Art towards the widest wideness but to ascend with it to the heights that climb towards the Highest is and must be part both of our aesthetic and our spiritual endeavour.

II

INTELLECTUAL THOUGHT, PHILOSOPHY AND POETRY

> *The modern trend in art, especially in poetry, has been towards laying a predominant stress on its thought-content. The modern mind asks of the poet not so much perfect beauty of song or of creative vision as a message to its seeking intelligence. The poet is expected to be not a supreme singer or an inspired seer but a philosopher, a prophet, a teacher, even something of a moral preacher. Is this not a deviation from the true function of poetry?*

This is only a sign of the intellectual malady of our age of which we are almost all of us the victims. The native power of poetry is in its sight, not in its intellectual thought-matter, and its safety is in adhering to this native principle of vision and allowing its conception, its thought, its emotions, its presentation, its structure to rise out of that or compelling it to rise into that before it takes its finished form. The poetic vision of life is not a critical or intellectual or philosophic view of it, but a soul-view, a seizing by the inner sense; and the Mantra is not in its substance or form poetic enunciation of a philosophic truth, but the rhythmic revelation or intuition arising out of the soul's sight of God and Nature and the world and the inner truth — occult to outward eye — of all that peoples it, the secrets of their life and being.

In claiming for the poet the role of a seer of Truth and in seeking the source of great poetry in a great and revealing vision of life or God or the gods or man or Nature, it is not meant that it is necessary for him to have an intellectual philosophy of life or a message for humanity, which he chooses to express in verse because he has the metrical gift and the gift of imagery, or a solution of the problems of the age or a mission to improve mankind, or, as it is said, "to leave the world better than he found it". As a man, he may have these things, but the less he allows them to get the better of his poetical gift, the happier it will be for his poetry. Material for his poetry they may give, an influence in it they may be, provided they are transmuted into vision and life by the poetical spirit, but they can be neither its soul nor its aim, nor give the law to its creative activity and its expression.

Are the functions of the poet and the philosopher then totally distinct?

The philosopher's business is to discriminate Truth and put its parts and aspects into intellectual relation with each other; the poet's is to seize and embody aspects of Truth in their living relations, or rather, — for that is too philosophical a language, — to see her features and excited by the vision create in the beauty of her image. The philosopher may bring in the aid of colour and image to give some relief and hue to his dry light of reason and water his arid path of abstractions with some healing dew of poetry. But these are ornaments and not the substance of his work; and if the philosopher makes his thought substance of poetry, he ceases to be a philosophical thinker and becomes a poet-seer of Truth. Thus the more rigid metaphysicians are perhaps right in denying to Nietzsche the name of philosopher; for Nietzsche does not think, but always sees, turbidly or clearly, rightly or distortedly, but with the eye of the seer rather than with the brain of the thinker. On the other hand, we may get great poetry which is largely or even wholly philosophic in its matter; but this philosophic poetry is poetry and lives as poetry only in so far as it departs from the method, the expression, the way of seeing proper to the philosophic mind. It must be vision pouring itself into thought-images and not thought trying to observe truth and distinguish.

In earlier days this distinction was not at all clearly understood and therefore we find even poets of great power attempting to set philosophic systems to music or even much more prosaic matter than a philosophic system, Hesiod and Virgil setting about even a manual of agriculture in verse! In Rome, always a little blunt of perception in the aesthetic mind, her

Intellectual Thought, Philosophy and Poetry 139

two greatest poets fell a victim to this unhappy conception, with results which are a lesson and a warning to all posterity. Lucretius' work lives only, in spite of the majestic energy behind it, by its splendid digressions into pure poetry, Virgil's Georgics by fine passages and pictures of Nature and beauties of word and image, but its substance is lifeless matter which has floated to us on the stream of Time saved for the beauty of its setting.

But in India the attempt at expressing philosophical thought in poetry has been successfully carried out in the Gita and the Upanishads. How was this possible?

India, and perhaps India alone, had managed once or twice to turn this kind of philosophic attempt into a poetic success, in the Gita, in the Upanishads and some minor works modelled upon them. But the difference is great. The Gita owes its poetical success to its starting from a great and critical situation in life, having that in view and always returning upon it, and to its method which is to seize on a spiritual experience or moment or stage of the inner life and throw it into the form of thought; and this, though a delicate operation, can keep well within the limits of the poetic manner of speech. Only where it overburdens itself with metaphysical matter and deviates into sheer philosophic definition and discrimination, which happens especially in two or three of its closing chapters, does the poetic voice sink under the weight, even occasionally into flattest versified prose. The Upanishads too, and much more, are not at all philosophic thinking, but spiritual seeing, a rush of spiritual intuitions throwing themselves inevitably into the language of poetry, shaped out of fire and life, because that is their natural speech and a more intellectual utterance would have falsified their vision.

Does this mean that there should be no philosophy in poetry or that the poet has no right to express philosophic thought or spiritual truth, as some critics have tried to maintain?

That depends on what is meant by "philosophy" in a poem. Of

course if one sets out to write a metaphysical argument in verse like the Greek Empedocles or the Roman Lucretius, it is a risky business and is likely to land you into prosaic poetry which is a less pardonable mixture than poetic prose. Even when philosophising in a less perilous way, one has to be careful not to be flat or heavy. It is obviously easier to be poetic when singing about a skylark than when one tries to weave a robe of verse to clothe the attributes of the Brahman. But that does not mean that there is to be no thought or no spiritual thought or no expression of truth in poetry; there is no great poet who has not tried to philosophise. Shelley wrote about the skylark, but he also wrote about the Brahman.

> Life, like a dome of many-coloured glass,
> Stains the white radiance of Eternity,

is as good poetry as

> *Hail to thee, blithe Spirit!*

There are flights of unsurpassable poetry in the Gita and the Upanishads. These rigid dicta are always excessive and there is no reason why a poet should allow the expression of his personality or the spirit within him or his whole poetic mind to be clipped, cabined or stifled by any theories or "thou shalt not"-s of this character. If the expression of philosophical truth in poetry is absolutely denied then half the world's poetry would have to disappear. Truth and Thought and Light cast into forms of beauty cannot be banished in that cavalier way. Music and art and poetry have striven from the beginning to express the vision of the deepest and greatest things and not the things of the surface only and it will be so as long as there are poetry and art and music. Philosophy has its place in poetry and can even take a leading place along with psychological experience as it does in the Gita. All depends on how it is done, whether it is a dry or a living philosophy, an arid intellectual statement or the expression not only of the living truth of thought but of something of its beauty, its light or its power.

III

SCIENCE, PHILOSOPHY, RELIGION AND POETRY

1. A. Richards in his book "Science and Poetry" tries to establish that the aim and function of science are altogether distinct from the aim and function of poetry. Science is concerned with the seeking of truth but poetry has nothing to do with the finding or expression of truth. He attaches very high value to the aesthetic experience which poetry yields but does not admit that it can in any way reveal to us truth. Is this true? As the poet can express in his own peculiar manner the truth of philosophy and religion, can he not also reveal in his distinct fashion the truth which the scientist discovers in his special field?

Infinite Truth has her many distinct ways of expressing and finding herself and each way must be kept distinct and the law of one must not be applied to the law of another form of her self-expression; and yet that does not mean that the material of one cannot be used as the material of another, though it must be cast by a different power into a different mould, or that all do not meet on their tops. Truth of poetry is not truth of philosophy or truth of science or truth of religion only, because it is another way of self-expression of infinite Truth so distinct that it appears to give quite another face of things and reveal quite another side of experience. A poet may have a religious creed or subscribe to a system of philosophy or take rank himself like Lucretius or certain Indian poets as a considerable philosophical thinker or succeed like Goethe as a scientist as well as a poetic creator, but the moment he begins to argue out his system intellectually in verse or puts up a dressed-up science straight into metre or else inflicts like Wordsworth or Dryden rhymed sermons or theological disputations on us, he is breaking the law. And even if he does not move so far astray, yet the farther he goes in that direction even within the bounds of his art, he is, though it has often been done with a tolerable, sometimes a considerable or total success, treading on unfirm or at any rate on lower ground. It is difficult for him there to maintain the authentic poetic spirit and pure inspiration.

What is the reason of this difficulty? Is it not possible for the poet to overcome this difficulty and present to us, though in a different way, the same essential truth of science, religion and philosophy?

This is another cult and worship and the moment the poet stands before the altar of the Muse, he has to change his robes of mind and serve the rites of a different consecration. He has to bring out into the front that other personality in him who looks with a more richly irised seeing eye and speaks with a more rapturous voice. The others have not normally the same joy of the word because they do not go to its fountain-head, even though each has its own intense delight, as philosophy has its joy of deep and comprehensive understanding and religion its hardly expressible rapture. Still it remains true that the poet may express precisely the same thing in essence as the philosopher or the man of religion or the man of science, may even give us truth of philosophy, truth of religion, truth of science, provided he transmutes it, abstracts from it something on which the others insist in their own special form and gives us the something more which poetic sight and expression bring. He has to convert it into truth of poetry, and it will be still better for his art if he saw it originally with the poetic insight, the creative, intuitive, directly perceiving and interpreting eye; for then his utterance of truth is likely to be more poetic, authentic, inspired and compelling. This distinction between poetic and other truth, well enough felt but not always well observed, and their fusion and meeting-place are worth dwelling upon; for if poetry is to do all it can for us in the new age, it will include increasingly in its scope much that will be common to it with philosophy, religion and even in a broader sense with science, and yet it will at the same time develop more intensely the special beauty and peculiar power of its own insight and its

Science, Philosophy, Religion and Poetry 143

own manner. The poetry of Tagore is already a new striking instance of what differently seen and followed out might have been a specifically philosophic and religious truth, but here turned into beauty and given a new significance by the transforming power of poetic vision.

What is the essential difference between the pursuits of the poet and the artist and those of the philosopher, the scientist and the religious seeker?

The difference which separates these great things of the mind is a difference of the principal, the indispensable instrument we must use and of the appeal to the mind and the whole manner. There is a whole gulf of difference. The philosopher sees in the dry light of the reason, proceeds dispassionately by a severe analysis and abstraction of the intellectual content of the truth, a logical slow close stepping from idea to pure idea, a method difficult and nebulous to the ordinary, hard, arid, impossible to the poetic mind. For the poetic mind sees at once in a flood of coloured light, in a moved experience, in an ecstasy of the coming of the word, in splendours of form, in a spontaneous leaping out of inspired idea upon idea, sparks of the hoof-beats of the white-flame horse Dadhikravan galloping up the mountain of the gods or breath and hue of wing beating upon wing of the irised broods of Thought flying over earth or up towards heaven. The scientist proceeds also by the intellectual reason but with a microscopic scrutiny which brings it to bear on an analysis of sensible fact and process and on the correct measure and relation of force and energy as it is seen working on the phenomenal stuff of existence, and joins continually link of fact with fact and coil of process with process till he has under his hand at least in skeleton and tissue the whole connected chain of apparent things. But to the poetic mind this is a dead mechanical thing; for the eye of the poet loves to look on breathing acting life in its perfected synthesis and rhythm, not on the constituent measures, still less on the dissected parts, and his look seizes the soul of wonder of things, not the mechanical miracle. The method of these other powers moves by the rigorously based and patiently self-assured steps of the systematising intelligence and the aspect of Truth which they uncover is a norm measured and cut out from the world of ideas and the world of sense by the eye of the intellectual reason. The brooding philosopher or the discovering scientist cannot indeed do without the aid of a greater power, intuition, but ordinarily he has to bring what that nearer, more swiftly luminous faculty gives him into a more deliberate air under the critical light of the intelligence and establish it in the dialectical or analytical way of philosophy and science before the intellect as judge. The mind of the poet sees by intuition and direct perception and brings out what they give him by a formative stress on the total image, and the aspect to which he thrills is the living truth of the form, of the life that inspires it, of the creative thought behind and the supporting movement of the soul and a rhythmic harmony of these things revealed to his delight in their beauty. These fields and paths lie very wide apart, and if any voices from the others reach and claim the ear of the poetic creator, they must change greatly in their form and suit themselves to the warmth and colour of his atmosphere before they can find right of entry into his kingdom.

But are these great pursuits of the human mind entirely different and separate? Is there no point where they meet?

Their meeting is not here at the base, but on the tops. The philosopher's reasoning intelligence discovers only a system of thought symbols and the reality they figure cannot be seized by the intelligence, but needs direct intuition, a living contact, a close experience by identity in our self of knowledge. That is work not for a dialectical, but a bright revelatory thinking, a luminous body of intuitive thought and spiritual experience which carries us straight into sight, into vision of knowledge. The first effort of philosophy is to know for the sake of pure understanding, but her greater height is to take Truth alive in the spirit and clasp and grow one with her and be consciously within ourselves all the reality we have learned to know. But that is precisely what the poet strives to do in his own way by intuition and imagination, when he labours to bring himself close to and be one by delight with the thing of beauty which awakes his joy. He does not always seize the very self of the thing, but to do so lies within his power. The language of intuitive thinking moves always therefore to an affinity with poetic speech and in the ancient Upanishads it used that commonly as its natural vehicle. "The Spirit went abroad, a thing pure, bright, unwounded by sin, without body or sinew or scar; the Seer, the Thinker, the Self-born who breaks into being all around us, decreed of old all things in their nature from long eternal years." "There sun shines not nor moon nor star nor these lightnings blaze nor this fire; all this world is luminous only with his light." Are we listening, one might ask, to the voice of poetry or philosophy or religion? It is all three voices cast in one, indistinguishable in the eternal choir. And there is too and similarly a pure intuitive science which comes into the field when we enter the ranges of the psychical and spiritual being and can from there work for the discovery of greater secrets of the physical or at least of the psycho-physical world. Indian Yoga founds itself on that great process, and there, though as in all true science the object is an assured method of personal discovery or living repetition and possession of past discovery and a working out of all the thing found, there is too a high final intention to hold the truth, the light found in our inner power of being and turn it to a power of our psychical self, our spirit, our self of knowledge and will, our self of love and joy, our self of life and action. This too, though not the same thing in form, is akin to the higher work of poetry when it acts, as the ancients would have had it consciously act, as a purifier and builder of the soul.

The initial function of religion again is to make clear the approaches of the soul to the Highest, to God. And it does that at first by laying on the mind a scheme of religious knowledge or guiding creed and dogma, a taming yoke of moral instruction or purifying law of religious conduct and an awakening call of religious emotion, worship, cult, and so far it is a thing apart in its own field, but in its truly revealing side of intuitive being and experience we find that the essence of religion is an aspiration and adoration of the soul towards the Divine, the Self, the Supreme, the Eternal, the Infinite, and an effort to get close to and live with or in that or to enjoy in love and be like or one with that which we adore. But poetry also on its heights turns to the same things in ourselves and the world, not indeed with religious adoration, but by a regarding closeness and moved oneness in beauty and delight. The characteristic method and first field of all these things is indeed wide apart, but at their end when they come into their deepest spirit, they begin to approach each other and touch; and because of this greater affinity philosophy, psychic and spiritual science and religion are found in the ancient Indian culture woven into one unity, and when they turn to the expression of their most intimate experience, it is always the poetic word which they use.

IV

POETRY AND LIFE

In recent years art and poetry have considerably freed themselves from the stress of intellectuality which so strongly dominated their seeing and expression in the nineteenth century and have turned more and more to the dynamic force of life for inspiration and creation. Is this a turn in the right direction?

The demand for life, for action, the tendency to a pragmatic and vitalistic view of things, a certain strenuous and even strident note has been loud enough in recent years. Life, action, vital power are great indispensable things, but to get back to them by thinking less is a way not open to us in this age of time, even if it were a desirable remedy for our disease of over-intellectuality and a mechanised existence. In fact we do not think less than the men of the past generation but much more insistently with a more packed and teeming thought, with a more eager, more absorbed hunting of the mind along all the royal high-roads and alluring byways of life. And it could not be otherwise. The very school of poetry which insists on actual life as the subject matter of the poet carries into it with or without conscious intention the straining of the thought-mind after something quite other than the obvious sense of the things it tries to force into relief, some significance deeper than what either the observing reason or the normal life-sense gives to our first or our second view of existence.

But is it not a fact that the predominance of the thinking intellect, however fruitful for the development of science and practical utilities, is very unfavourable to the creation of art and poetry and that a turning towards life is essential to restore their creative vigour?

The intellect moves naturally between two limits, the abstractions or solving analyses of the reason and the domain of positive and practical reality; its great achievements are in these two fields or in a mediation between them, and it can do most and go farthest, can achieve its most native and characteristic and therefore its greatest and completest work either in philosophy or in science. The age of developed intellectualism in Greece killed poetry; it ended in the comedy of Menander, the intellectual artificialities of Alexandrianism, the last flush of beauty in the aesthetic pseudo-naturalism of the Sicilian pastoral poetry; philosophy occupied the field. In the more rich and complex modern mind this result could not so easily come and has not yet come. At the same time the really great, perfect and securely characteristic work of the age has not been in the field of art and poetry, but in critical thought and science. Criticism and science, by a triumphant force of abstraction and analysis turned on the world of positive fact, have in this period been able to become enormously effective for life. They have been able to reign sovereignly, not so much by their contributions to pure knowledge, but by their practical, revolutionary and constructive force. If modern thought with its immense scientific achievement has not enriched life at its base or given it a higher and purer action, — it has only created a yet unrealised possibility in that direction by its idealistic side, — it has wonderfully equipped it with powerful machinery and an imposing paraphernalia and wrought conspicuous and unprecedented changes in its superstructure. But poetry in this atmosphere has kept itself alive not by any native and spontaneous power born of agreement between its own essential spirit and the spirit of the age, but by a great effort of the imagination and aesthetic intelligence labouring for the most part to make the best of what material it could get in the shape of new thought and new viewpoints for the poetic criticism or the thoughtful presentation of life. It has been an aesthetic by-play rather than a leading or sometimes even premier force in the cultural life of the race such as it was in the ancient ages and even, with a certain limited action, in more recent times.

Does this mean that there is a basic incompatibility between intellect and poetry?

The pure intellect cannot create poetry. The inspired or the imaginative reason does indeed play an important, sometimes a leading part, but even that can only be a support or an influence; the thinking mind may help to give a final shape, a great and large form, *Saṁmahemā manīṣayā,* as the Vedic poets said of the Mantra, but the word must start first from a more intimate sense in the heart of the inner being, *hrrda tassttaan;* it is the spirit within and not the mind without that is the fount of poetry. Poetry too is an interpreter of truth, but in the forms of an innate beauty, and not so much of intellectual truth, the truths offered by the critical mind, as of the intimate truth of being. It deals not so much with things thought as with things seen, not with the authenticities of the analytic mind, but with the authenticities of the synthetic vision and the seeing spirit. The abstractions, generalisations, minute precisions of our ordinary intellectual cerebration are not part of its essence or texture; but it has others, more luminous, more subtle, those which come to us after passing through the medium and getting drenched in the light of the intuitive and revealing mind. And therefore when the general activity of thought runs predominantly into the former kind, the works of the latter are apt to proceed under rather anaemic conditions, they are affected by the pervading atmosphere; poetry either ceases or falls into a minor strain or takes refuge in virtuosities of its outer instruments and aids or, if it still does any considerable work, lacks the supreme spontaneity, the natural perfection, the sense of abundant ease or else of sovereign mastery which the touch of the spirit manifests even amidst the fullest or austerest labour of its creation.

Can poetry really overcome this limitation by refraining altogether from thinking and turning solely to life? Is it not possible to harmonise thought and life at a higher level and make them both authentic powers for poetic creation?

The way out lies not in cessation of thinking and the turn to a strenuous description of life, nor even in a more vitally forceful thinking, but in another kind of thought-mind. The filled activity of the thinking mind is as much part of life as that of the body and vital and emotional being, and its growth and predominance are a necessary stage of human progress and man's self-evolution. To go back from it is impossible or, if possible, would be undesirable, a lapse and not a betterment of our spirit. But the full thought-life does not come by the activity of the intellectual reason and its predominance. That is only a step by which we get above the first immersion in the activity and excitement and vigour of the life and the body and give ourselves a first freedom to turn to a greater and higher reach of the fullness of existence. And that higher reach we gain when we get above the limited crude physical mind, above the vital power and its forceful thought and self-vision, above the intellect and its pondering and measuring reason, and tread the illumined realm of an intuitive and spiritual thinking, an intuitive feeling, sense and vision. This is not that vital intuition which is sometimes confused with a much broader, loftier, vaster and more seeing power, but the high original power itself, a supra-intellectual and spiritual intuition. The all-informing spirit, when found in all its fullness, heals the scission between thought and life, the need of a just balance between them disappears, instead there begins a new and luminous and joyful fusion and oneness. The spirit gives us not only a greater light of truth and vision, but the breath of a greater living; for the spirit is not only the self of our consciousness and knowledge, but the great self of life. To find our self and the self of things is not to go through a rarefied ether of thought into Nirvana, but to discover the whole greatest integral power of our complete existence.

V

REALISM IN ART AND POETRY

Art and poetry in recent years, especially amongst people influenced by communistic ideology, have concerned themselves almost exclusively with real and actual life. Any preoccupation with things that have no direct, real and near contact with actual life is decried as going after unsubstantial and shadowy illusions or remote and airy imaginations and fancies of no value to the individual or the race. How far is this insistence on realism compatible with the true function and aim of art and poetry?

The demand for activity and realism or for a direct, exact and forceful presentation of life in poetry proceeds upon a false sense of what poetry gives or can give us. All the highest activities of the mind of man deal with things other than the crude actuality or the direct appearance or the first rough appeal of existence. A critical or a scientific thought may attempt to give an account of the actuality as it really is, though even to do that they have to go far behind its frontage and make a mental reconstruction and surprising change in its appearance. But the creative powers cannot stop there, but have to make new things for us as well as to make existing things new to the mind and eye. It is no real portion of the function of art to cut out palpitating pieces from life and present them raw and smoking or well-cooked for the aesthetic digestion. For in the first place all art has to give us beauty, and the crude actuality of life is not often beautiful, and in the second place poetry has to give us a deeper reality of things and the outsides and surface faces of life are only a part of its reality and do not take us either very deep or very far. Moreover, the poet's greatest work is to open to us new realms of vision, new realms of being, our own and the world's, and he does this even when he is dealing with actual things.

> *But is it not a fact that some of the greatest poets like Homer and Shakespeare depict faithfully the actual events and personalities of their time in the themes and characters of their work?*

Homer with all his epic vigour of outward presentation does not show us the heroes and deeds before Troy in their actuality as they really were to the normal vision of men, but much rather as they were or might have been to the vision of the gods. Shakespeare's greatness lies not in his reproduction of actual human events or men as they appear to us buttoned and cloaked in life, — others of his time could have done that as well, if with less radiant force of genius, yet with more of the realistic crude colour or humdrum drab of daily truth, — but in his bringing out in his characters and themes of things essential, intimate, eternal, universal in man and Nature and Fate on which the outward features are borne as fringe and robe and which belong to all times, but are least obvious to the moment's experience: when we do see them, life presents to us another face and becomes something deeper than its actual present mask. That is why the poet oftenest instinctively prefers to go away from the obsession of a petty actuality, from the realism of the prose of life to his inner creative self or an imaginative background of the past or the lucent air of myth or dream or on into a greater outlook on the future.

> *Does this mean that art and poetry should turn away from the immediate actualities of life and deal mainly with things of universal and eternal interest?*

Poetry may indeed deal with the present living scene, at some peril, or even with the social or other questions and problems of the day, — a task which is now often laid on the creative mind, as if that were its proper work; but it does that successfully only when it makes as little as possible of what belongs to the moment and time and the surface and brings out their roots of universal or eternal interest or their suggestion of great and deep things. What the poet borrows from the moment, is the most perishable part of his work and lives at all only by being subordinated and put into intimate relation with less transient realities. And this is so because it is the eternal soul of man and the intimate self of things and their more abiding and significant forms which are the real object of his vision.

Is it likely that the poetry of the future, in recovering its complete aim and purpose, will outgrow its present preoccupation with the surface actualities of normal life and widen its scope by entering into the vaster realms of the greater life of the Spirit?

The poetry of the future can least afford to chain itself to the outward actualities which we too often mistake for the whole of life, because it will be the voice of a human mind which is pressing more and more towards the very self of the self of things, the very spirit of which the soul of man is a living power and to a vision of unity and totality which is bound to take note of all that lies behind our apparent material life. What man sees and experiences of God and himself and his race and Nature and the spiritual, mental, psychic and material worlds in which he moves, his backlook upon the past, his sweep of vision over the present, his eye of aspiration and prophecy cast towards the future, his passion of self-finding and self-exceeding, his reach beyond the three times to the eternal and immutable, this is his real life.

But poetry in the past has already sung of this greater life of the Spirit, of God and the gods and other worlds and the deeper truths of Nature and man's life. Will the poetry of the future in returning to these subjects only repeat the visions and the voices of the past or give us a new interpretation of them?

Poetry in the past wrote much of the godheads and powers behind existence, but in the mask of legends and myths, sometimes of God, but not often with a living experience, oftener in the set forms taught by religions and churches and without true beauty and knowledge. But now the mind of man is opening more largely to the deepest truth of the Divine, the Self, the Spirit, the eternal Presence not separate and distant, but near us, around us and in us, the Spirit in the world, the greater Self in man and his kind, the Spirit in all that is and lives, the Godhead, the Existence, the Power, the Beauty, the eternal Delight that broods over all, supports all and manifests itself in every turn of creation. A poetry which lives in this vision must give us quite a new presentation and interpretation of life; for of itself and at the first touch this seeing reconstructs and re-images the world for us and gives us a greater sense and a vaster, subtler and profounder form of our existence. The real faces of the gods are growing more apparent to the eye of the mind, though not yet again intimate with our life, and the forms of legend and symbol and myth must open to other and deeper meanings, as already they have begun to do, and come in changed and vital again into poetry to interpret the realities behind the veil. Nature wears already to our eye a greater and more transparent robe of her divine and her animal and her terrestrial and cosmic life and a deeper poetry of Nature than has yet been written is one of the certain potentialities of the future. The material realm too cannot for very much longer be our sole or separate world of experience, for the partitions which divide it from psychic and other kingdoms behind it are wearing thin and voices and presences are beginning to break through and reveal their impact on our world. This too must widen our conception of life and make a new world and atmosphere for poetry which may justify as perhaps never before the poet's refusal to regard as unreal what to the normal mind was only romance, illusion or dream. A larger field of being made more real to man's experience will be the realm of the future poetry.

But why has the modern mind considered these greater realms of the life of the Spirit as unreal dreams or illu-

sions? Are they not as real as the world of our normal experience?

These things are often given an appearance of remoteness, of withdrawal from the actuality of life, because to discover them the mind had at first to draw away from the insistent outward preoccupation and live as if in a separate world. The seeker of the Self and Spirit, the God-lover, tended to become the cloistered monk, the ascetic, the mystic, the eremite and to set the spiritual apart from and against the material life. The lover of Nature went away from the noise of man and daily things to commune with her largeness and peace. The gods were found more in the lights of solitude than in the thoughts and actions of man. The seer of other worlds lived surrounded by the voices and faces of supernature. And this was a legitimate seclusion, for these are provinces and realms and presences and one has often to wander apart in them or live secluded with them to know their nearest intimacies. The spirit is real in itself even apart from the world, the gods have their own home beyond our sky and air, Nature her own self-absorbed life and supernature its brilliant curtains and its dim mysterious fences. None of these things are unreal, and if the supernatural as handled by older poets seemed often mere legend, fancy and romance, it was because it was seen from a distance by the imagination, not lived in by the soul and in its spirit, as is done by the true seer and poet of this supernature or other-nature. And all these things, because they have their own reality, have their life and a poetry which makes them its subject, can be as vital, as powerful, as true as the song which makes beautiful the physical life and normal passions and emotions of men and the objects of our bodily sense-experience.

But is it not likely that the poetry of the future in its preoccupation with the greater truths of the super-life and the vaster realms of supernature may tend to belittle our normal actual life and even give it a hue of unreality just as modern poetry in its preoccupation with our actual life has belittled and treated as unreal the greater life of the spirit and the higher worlds of supernature?

But all life is one and a new human mind moves towards the realisation of its totality and oneness. The poetry which voices the oneness and totality of our being and Nature and the worlds and God, will not make the actuality of our earthly life less but more real and rich and full and wide and living to men. To know other countries is not to belittle but enlarge our own country and help it to a greater power of its own being, and to know the other countries of the soul is to widen our bounds and make more opulent and beautiful the earth on which we live. To bring the gods into our life is to raise it to its own diviner powers. To live in close and abiding intimacy with Nature and the spirit in her is to free our daily living from its prison of narrow preoccupation with the immediate moment and act and to give the moment the inspiration of all Time and the background of eternity and the daily act the foundation of an eternal peace and the large momentum of the universal Power. To bring God into life, the sense of the self in us into all our personality and becoming, the powers and vistas of the Infinite into our mental and material existence, the oneness of the self in all into our experience and feelings and relations of heart and mind with all that is around us is to help to divinise our actual being and life, to force down its fences of division and blindness and unveil the human godhead: that individual man and his race can become if they will and lead us to our most vital perfection. This is what a future poetry may do for us in the way and measure in which poetry can do these things, by vision, by the power of the word, by the attraction of the beauty and delight of what it shows us. What philosophy or other mental brooding makes precise or full to our thought, poetry can by its creative power, imaging force and appeal to the emotions make living to the soul and heart. This poetry will present to us indeed in forms of power and beauty all the actual life of man, his wonderful and fruitful past, his living and striving present, his yet more living aspiration and hope of the future, but will present it more seeingly as the life of the vast self and spirit within the race and the veiled divinity in the individual, as an act of the power and delight of universal being, in the greatness of an eternal manifestation, in the presence and intimacy of Nature, in harmony with the beauty and wonder of the realms that stretch out beyond earth and its life, in the march to godhead and the significance of immortality, in the ever clear letters and symbols of the self-revealing mystery and not only in its first crude and incomplete actualities; these actualities will themselves be treated with a firmer and finer vision, find their own greater meaning and become to our sight thread of the fine tissue and web of the cosmic work of the Spirit. This poetry will be the voice and rhythmic utterance of our greater, our total, our infinite existence, and will give us the strong and infinite sense, the spiritual and vital joy, the exalting power of a greater breath of life.

VI

DECADENCE IN MODERN ART AND LITERATURE

Much of the recent work in art, literature and poetry has been condemned by some critics as decadent. What is meant by decadence in literature and art and how does it come about?

Literature and art become decadent when the race decays, when life and soul go out and only the dry intellect and tired senses remain. Decadence arrives when in the decline of a culture there is nothing more to be lived or seen or said, or when the creative mind settles irretrievably into a clumsy and artificial repetition of past forms and conventions or can only escape from them into scholastic or aesthetic pettinesses or extravagance.

Is the charge of decadence levelled against modern art and poetry valid?

That a certain decline, not of the activity of the poetic mind, but of its natural vigour, importance and effective power has been felt, if not quite clearly appreciated in its causes, we can see from various significant indications. Throughout the later nineteenth century one observes a constant apprehension of approaching aesthetic decadence, a tendency to be on the lookout for it and to find the signs of it in innovations and new turns in art and poetry. The attempt to break the whole mould of poetry and make a new thing of it so that it may be easier to handle and may shape itself to all the turns, the high and low, noble and common, fair or unseemly movements of the modern mind and its varied interest in life, is itself due to a sense of some difficulty, limitation and unease, some want of equation between the fine but severely self-limiting character of this kind of creative power and the spirit of the age. At one time indeed it was hardly predicted that since the modern mind is increasingly scientific and less and less poetically and aesthetically imaginative, poetry must necessarily decline and give place to science, — for much the same reason, in fact, for which philosophy replaced poetry in Greece. On the opposite side it was sometimes suggested that the poetic mind might become more positive and make use of the materials of science or might undertake a more intellectual though always poetic criticism of life and might fill the place of philosophy and religion which were supposed for a time to be dead or dying powers in human nature; but this came to the same thing, for it meant a deviation from the true law of aesthetic creation and only a more protracted decadence.

What was the chief reason of this decadence?

An age of reason dominated by the critical, philosophic or scientific intelligence is ordinarily unfavourable and, even when it is most catholic and ample, cannot be quite favourable to great poetic creation. Intellectualism, if it leads to nothing beyond itself must end, however brilliant its work, in a poetic decadence, and that must come nearer, the more intellect dominates the other powers of our being. The turn of poetry in the age which we have now left behind, was, as was inevitable in a reign of dominant intellectuality, a pre-occupation with reflective thought and therefore with truth, but it was not at its core and in its essence poetic thought and truth and its expression, however artistically dressed with image and turn or enforced by strong or dexterous phrase, however frequently searching, apt or picturesque, had not often, except in one or two exceptional voices, the most moving and intimate tones of poetry. The poets of the middle nineteenth century in England and America philosophised, moralised or criticised life in energetic and telling or beautiful and attractive or competent and cultured verse; but they did not represent life with success or interpret it with high poetic power or inspired insight and were not stirred and uplifted by any deeply great vision of truth. The reasoning and observing intellect is a most necessary and serviceable instrument, but an excess of reason and intellectuality does not create an atmosphere favourable to moved vision and the uplifting breath of life, and for all its great stir of progress and discovery, that age, the carnival of industry and science, gives us who are in search of more living, inner and potent things the impression of a brazen flavour, a heavy air, an inhibition of the greater creative movements, a level spirit of utility and prose. The few poets who strained towards a nearer hold upon life, had to struggle against this atmosphere which weighed upon their mind and clogged their breath. Whitman, striving by stress of thought towards a greater truth of the soul and life, found refuge in a revolutionary breaking out into new anarchic forms, a vindication of freedom of movement which unfortunately at its ordinary levels brings us nearer to the earth and not higher up towards a more illumined air; Swinburne, excited by the lyric fire within him, had too often to lash himself into a strained violence of passion in order to make a way through the clogging thickness for its rush of sound; Meredith's strains, hymning life in a word burdened and packed with thought, are strong and intimate, but difficult and few. And therefore in this epoch of a bursting into new fields and seeking for new finer and bolder impulses of creation, one of the most insistent demands and needs of the human mind, not only in poetry, but in thought itself and in spirit, has been to lessen the tyranny of the reasoning and critical intellect, to return to the power and sincerity of life and come by a greater deepness of the intuition of its soul of meaning. That is the most striking turn of all recent writing of any importance.

> *But though the urge behind this turn was in itself sound, can it be said that it proceeded in the right direction and succeeded in laying hold on a greater truth of life and thereby bridging the gulf between thought and life created by the over-intellectuality of the modern age? The earlier poetry of the pre-intellectual period even though it moved in the sphere of external life and its passions and emotions had fullness of vitality and natural wholeness, but much of*

the recent poetry is perverse, morbid or unsound. What is the reason of this?

In the intellectual age passion, direct feeling, ardent emotion, sincerity of sensuous joy are chilled by the observing eye of the reason and give place to a play of sentiment, — sentiment which is an indulgence of the intelligent observing mind in the aesthesis, the *rasa* of feeling, passion, emotion, sense, thinning them away into a subtle, at the end almost unreal fineness. There is then an attempt to get back to the natural fullness of the vital and physical life, but the endeavour fails in sincerity and success because it is impossible; the mind of man having got so far cannot return upon its course, undo what it has made of itself and recover glad childhood of its early vigorous nature. There is instead of the simplicity of spontaneous life, a search after things striking, exaggerated, abnormal, violent, new, in the end a morbid fastening on perversities, on all that is ugly, glaring and coarse on the plea of their greater reality, on exaggerations of vital instinct and sensation, on physical wrynesses and crudities and things unhealthily strange. The thought-mind, losing the natural full-blooded power of the vital being, pores on these things, stimulates the failing blood with them and gives itself an illusion of some forceful sensation of living. This is not the real issue, but the way to exhaustion and decadence.

How can poetry avoid this exhaustion and decadence? What is the new direction in which it must turn to find the true way out of this false deviation?

The truth which poetry expresses takes two forms, the truth of life and the truth of that which works in life, the truth of the inner spirit. It may take its stand on the outer life and work in an intimate identity, relation or close dwelling upon it, and then what it does is to bring some life of intuitive things, some power of revelation of the beauty that is truth and the truth that is beauty into the outer things of life, even into those that are most common, obvious, of daily occurrence. But also it may get back into the truth of the inner spirit and work in an intimate identity, relation or close dwelling upon it, and then what it will do is to give a new revelation of our being and life and thought and nature and the material and the psychical and spiritual worlds. That is the effort to which it seems to be turning now in its most characteristic, effective and beautiful manifestations. But it cannot fully develop in this sense unless the general mind of the age takes that turn. There are signs that this will indeed be the outcome of the new direction taken by the modern mind, not an intellectual petrification or a long spinning in the grooves of a critical intellectualism, but a higher and more authentic thinking and living. The human intelligence seems to be on the verge of an attempt to rise through the intellectual into an intuitive mentality; it is no longer content to regard the intellect and the world of positive fact as all or the intellectual reason as a sufficient mediator between life and the spirit, but is beginning to perceive that there is a spiritual mind which can admit us to a greater and more comprehensive vision. This does not mean any sacrifice of the gains of the past, but a raising and extending of them not only by a seeking of the inner as well as the outer truth of things, but also of all that binds them together and a bringing of them into true relation and oneness. An age which brings in large and new vital and spiritual truths, truths of our being, truths of the self of man and the inner self of Nature and opens vast untrod ranges to sight and imagination, is not likely to be an age of decadence, and a poetry which voices these things, — unless its creative power has been fatally atrophied by long conventionalism, and that is not at present our case, — is not likely to be a poetry of decadence.

VII

SURREALIST ART AND POETRY (1)

There is a strong tendency in modern art and poetry to seek for bare simplicity and directness as can be seen in the poetry of D.H. Lawrence and certain new movements in art like cubism, surrealism, abstract painting, etc. What is the basic idea behind this tendency?

The idea is to get rid of all over-expression, of language for the sake of language, or form for the sake of form, even of indulgence of poetic emotion for the sake of the emotion, because all that veils the thing in itself, dresses it up, prevents it from coming out in the seizing nudity of its truth, the power of its intrinsic appeal. There is a sort of mysticism here that wants to express the inexpressible, the concealed, the invisible. Reduce expression to its barest bareness and you get nearer the inexpessible; suppress as much of the form as may be and you get nearer that behind, which is invisible. It is the same impulse that has pervaded recent endeavours in Art. Form hides, not expresses the reality; let us suppress the concealing form and express the reality by its appropriate geometrical figures — and you have cubism. Or since that is too much, suppress exactitude of form and replace it by more significant forms that indicate rather than conceal the truth — so you have "abstract" paintings. Or, what is within reveals itself in dreams not in waking phenomena, let us have in poetry or painting the figures, visions, sequences, designs of Dream — and you have surrealist art and poetry. The idea of Lawrence is akin: let us get rid of rhyme, metre, artifices which please us for their own sake and draw us away from the thing in itself, the real behind the form. So suppressing these things let us have something bare, rocky, primally expressive.

Is this idea quite sound? Has it been worked out with success in the creations of modern poets?

There is nothing to find fault with in the theory provided it does lead to a new creation which expresses the inner truth in things better and more vividly and directly than with its rhyme and metre, the old poetry, now condemned as artificial and rhetorical, succeeded in expressing it. But the results do not come up to expectation. What the modern metreless verse does is to catch up the movements of prose and try to fit them into varying or variously arranged lengths of verse. Sometimes something which has its own beauty or power is done — though nothing better or even equal to the best that was done before, but for the most there is either an easy or a strained ineffectiveness.

Does this mean that new metrical forms are bound to prove a failure and should not be attempted?

It does not follow that new and free forms are not to be attempted or that they cannot succeed at all. But if they succeed it will be by bringing the fundamental quality, power, movement of the old poetry — which is the eternal quality of all poetry — into new metrical and rhythmical discoveries and new secrets of poetic expression. It cannot be done by reducing these to skeletonic bareness or suppressing them by subdual and dilution in a vain attempt to unite the free looseness of prose with the gathered and intent paces of poetry.

Surrealism has been the most influential of all modern movements in art and poetry. The theory and aim of this movement is differently explained by different critics. What is its true aim and significance?

Surrealism is part of an increasing attempt of the European mind to escape from the surface consciousness (in poetry as well as in painting and in thought) and grope after a deeper truth of things which is not on the surface. The dream consciousness as it is called — meaning not merely what we see in dreams but the inner consciousness in which we get into contact with deeper worlds which underlie, influence and to some extent explain much in our lives, what the psychologists call the subliminal or the subconscient (the latter a very ambiguous phrase) — offers the first road of escape and the surrealists seem to be trying to force it. My impression is that there is much fumbling and that more often it is obscure and not always very safe layers that are tapped. That accounts for the note of diabolism that comes in in Baudelaire, in Rimbaud also, I believe, and in certain ugly elements in English surrealist poetry and painting. But this is only an impression.

What is the explanation of so much obscurity and unintelligibility in surrealist poetry and art? Is it its deliberate aim to remain obscure and unintelligible as some critics like Housman try to maintain?

Obscurity and unintelligibility are not the essence of any poetry and — except for unconscious or semi-conscious humorists like Dadaists — cannot be its aim or principle. True dream-poetry (let us call it so for the nonce) has and must always have a meaning and a coherence. But it may very well be obscure or seem meaningless to those who take their stand on the surface or "waking" mind and accept only its links and logic. Dream-poetry is usually full of images, visions, symbols that seek to strike at things too deep for the ordinary means of expression. N does not deliberately make his poems obscure; he writes what comes through from the source he has tapped and does not interfere with its flow by his own mental volition. In many modernist poets there may be labour and a deliberate posturing, but it is not so in his case. I interpret his poems because he wants me to do it, but I have always told him that an intellectual rendering narrows the meaning — it has to be seen and felt, not thought out. Thinking it out may give a satisfaction and an appearance of mental logicality, but the deeper sense and sequence can only be apprehended by an inner sense. I myself do not try to find out the meaning of his poems, I try to feel what they mean in vision and experience and then render into mental terms. This is a special kind of poetry and has to be dealt with according to its kind and nature. There is a sequence, a logic, a design in them, but not one that can satisfy the more rigid law of the logical intelligence.

About Housman's theory: it is not merely an appeal to emotion that he posits as the test of pure poetry; he deliberately says that pure poetry does not bother about intellectual meaning at all, it is to the intellect, nonsense. He says that the interpretations of Blake's famous poems rather spoil them — they appeal better without being dissected in that way. His theory is questionable, but that is what it comes to; he is wrong in using the word "nonsense" and perhaps in speaking of pure and impure poetry. All the same, to Blake and to writers of the dream-consciousness, his rejection of the intellectual standard is quite applicable.

VIII

SURREALIST ART AND POETRY (2)

Though it is true that the productions of the surrealist art and poetry often appear to us incoherent and meaningless only because our surface mind has not the right clue to interpret the sense of the designs, symbols and sequences of the transcriptions of the surrealist dream-experiences, still is it not a fact that some of these experiences are themselves incoherent, confused, pointless and ugly? What is the explanation of this?

If the surrealist dream-experiences are flat, pointless or ugly, it must be because they penetrate only as far as the "subconscious" physical and "subconscious" vital dream layers which are the strata nearest to the surface. Dream-consciousness is a vast world in which there are a multitude of provinces and kingdoms, but ordinary dreamers for the most part penetrate consciously only to these first layers which belong to what may properly be called the subconscious belt. When they pass into deeper sleep regions, their recording surface dream-mind becomes unconscious and no longer gives any transcript of what is seen and experienced there; or else in coming back, these experiences of the deeper strata fade away and are quite forgotten before one reaches the waking state. But when there is a stronger dream-capacity, or the dream-state becomes more conscious, then one is aware of these deeper experiences and can bring back a transcript which is sometimes a clear record, sometimes a hieroglyph, but in either case possessed of a considerable interest and significance.

It is only the subconscious belt that is chaotic in its dream sequences, for its transcriptions are fantastic and often mixed, combining a jumble of different elements: some play with impressions from the past, some translate outward touches on the sleep-mind; most are fragments from successive dream experiences that are not really part of one connected experience —

as if a gramophone record were to be made up of snatches of different songs all jumbled together. The vital dreams even in the subconscious range are often coherent in themselves and only seem incoherent to the waking intelligence because the logic and law of their sequences is different from the logic and law which the physical reason imposes on the incoherences of physical life. But if one gets the guiding clue and if one has some dream-experience and dream-insight, then it is possible to seize the links of the sequences and make out the significance, often very profound or very striking, both of the detail and of the whole. Deeper in, we come to perfectly coherent dreams recording the experience of the inner vital and inner mental planes; there are also true psychic dreams — the latter usually are of a great beauty.

What change does our dream-experience undergo in passing from the nearer layers of the subconscious to the deeper ranges of our subliminal self?

If the subliminal thus comes to the front in our dream consciousness, there is sometimes an activity of our subliminal intelligence, — dream becomes a series of thoughts, often strangely or vividly figured, problems are solved which our waking consciousness could not solve, warnings, premonitions, indications of the future, veridical dreams replace the normal subconscious incoherence. There can come also a structure of symbol images, some of a mental character, some of a vital nature: the former are precise in their figures, clear in their significance; the latter are often complex and baffling to our waking consciousness, but, if we can seize the clue, they reveal their own sense and peculiar system of coherence. Finally, there can come to us the records of happenings seen or experienced by us on other planes of our own being or of universal being into which we enter: these have sometimes, like the symbolic dreams, a strong bearing on our own inner and outer life or the life of others, reveal elements of our or their mental being and life-being or disclose influences on them of which our waking self is totally ignorant; but sometimes they have no such bearing and are purely records of other organised systems of consciousness independent of our physical existence. The subconscious dreams constitute the bulk of our most ordinary sleep-experience and they are those which we usually remember; but sometimes the subliminal builder is able to impress our sleep consciousness sufficiently to stamp his activities on our waking memory. If we develop our inner being, live more inwardly than most men do, then the balance is changed and a larger dream-consciousness opens before us; our dreams can take on a subliminal and no longer a subconscious character and can assume a reality and significance.

What is the difference between our subconscious and subliminal selves and how are they related to our surface waking self?

The subconscious in us is the extreme border of our secret inner existence where it meets the Inconscient, it is a degree of our being in which the Inconscient struggles into a half consciousness; the surface physical consciousness also, when it sinks back from the waking level and retrogresses towards the Inconscient, retires into this intermediate subconscience. Or, from another viewpoint, this nether part of us may be described as the antechamber of the Inconscient through which its formations rise into our waking or our subliminal being. When we sleep and the surface physical part of us, which is in its first origin here an output from the Inconscient, relapses towards the originating inconscience, it enters into this subconscious element, antechamber or substratum, and there it finds the impressions of its past or persistent habits of mind and experiences, — for all have left their mark on our subconscious part and have there a power of recurrence. In its effect on our waking self this recurrence often takes the form of a reassertion of old habits, impulses dormant or suppressed, rejected elements of the nature, or it comes up as some other not so easily recognisable, some peculiar disguised or subtle result of these suppressed or rejected but not erased impulses or elements.

Our subliminal self is not, like our surface physical being, an outcome of the energy of the Inconscient; it is a meeting-place of the consciousness that emerges from below by evolution and the consciousness that has descended from above for involution. There is in it an inner mind, an inner vital being of ourselves, an inner or subtle-physical being larger than our outer being and nature. This inner existence is the concealed origin of almost all in our surface self that is not a construction of the first inconscient World-Energy or a natural developed functioning of our surface consciousness or a reaction of it to impacts from the outside universal Nature, — and even in this construction, these functionings, these reactions, the subliminal takes part and exercises on them a considerable influence. There is here a consciousness which has a power of direct contact with the universal unlike the mostly indirect contacts which our surface being maintains with the universe through the sense-mind and the senses. There are here inner senses, a subliminal sight, touch, hearing; but these subtle senses are rather channels of the inner being's direct consciousness of things than its informants: the subliminal is not dependent on its senses for its knowledge, they only give a form to its direct experience of objects; they do not, so much as in a waking mind, convey forms of objects for the mind's documentation or as the starting-point or basis for an indirect constructive experience. The subliminal has the right of entry into the mental and vital and subtle-physical planes of the universal consciousness, it is not confined to the material plane and the physical world; it possesses means of communication with the worlds of being which the descent towards involution created in its passage and with all corresponding planes or worlds that may have arisen or been constructed to serve the purpose of the re-ascent from Inconscience to Superconscience. It is into this large realm of interior existence that our mind and vital being retire when they withdraw from the surface activities whether by sleep or inward-drawn concentration or by the inner plunge of trance.

Our waking state is unaware of its connection with the subliminal being, although it receives from it — but without any knowledge of the place of origin — the inspirations, intuitions, ideas, will-suggestions, sense-suggestions, urges to action that rise from below or from behind our limited surface existence. Sleep like trance opens the gate of the subliminal to us; for in sleep, as in trance, we retire behind the veil of the limited waking personality and it is behind this veil that the subliminal has its existence. But we receive the records of our sleep experience through dream and in dream figures and not in that condition which might be called an inner waking and which is the most accessible form of the trance state, nor through the supernormal clarities of vision and other more luminous and concrete ways of communication developed by the inner subliminal cognition when it gets into habitual or occasional conscious connection with our waking self. The subliminal, with the subconscious as an annexe of itself, — for the subconscious is also part of the behind-the-veil entity, — is the seer of inner things and of supraphysical experiences; the surface subconscious is only a transcriber. It is for this reason that the Upanishad describes the subliminal being as the Dream Self because it is normally in dreams, visions, absorbed states of inner experience that we enter into and are part of its experiences, — just as it describes the superconscient as the Sleep Self because normally all mental or sensory experiences cease when we enter this superconscience.

> *All artists (except those who insist on being crudely realistic) make free use of their imagination in dealing with the subject-matter of their art. Is such a free use of imagination permissible in the case of surrealist art or poetry which is largely a transcription of the dream experiences on the deeper levels of consciousness?*

It depends on the nature of the dreams. If they are of the right kind, they need no aid of imagination to be converted into poetry. If they are significant, imagination in the sense of a free use of mental invention might injure their truth and meaning — unless of course the imagination is of the nature of an inspired vision coming from the same plane and filling out or reconstructing the recorded experience so as to bring out the Truth held in it more fully than the dream transcript could do; for a dream record is usually compressed and often hastily selective.

IX

ART AND THE COMMON MAN — SUBJECTIVE ELEMENT IN APPRECIATION OF ART

The growth of democratic and socialistic tendencies in recent years have everywhere raised the demand of bringing down art and poetry, which had previously remained confined to the cultured few, to the general mass of humanity, or "the man in the street" as he is called. Only that art and poetry is considered valuable which appeals to the taste of the common man and can be easily understood by him; all the rest which it is difficult for him to appreciate without special training or which does not appeal to his uncultivated tastes is dismissed as meaningless moonshine or a useless extravagance. How far is this demand justifiable?

I do not know why so much value is put on general understanding and acceptance. Really it is only the few that can be trusted to discern the true value of things in poetry and art and if the "general" run accept, it is usually because acceptance is sooner or later imposed or induced in their minds by the authority of the few and afterwards by the verdict of Time. There are exceptions, of course, of a wide spontaneous acceptance because something that is really good happens to suit a taste or a demand in the general mind of the moment. Poetic and artistic value does not necessarily command mass understanding and acceptance. Moreover, the majority of minds do not respond to "artistic" beauty at all — something inartistic appeals much more to what sense of beauty they have — or else they are not seeking beauty, but only vital pleasure.

Why is the work of a poet or an artist differently estimated by different critics? Sometimes a poet or artist is praised in the highest terms by some eminent critics and condemned outright by other equally eminent critics. What is the explanation for this?

All criticism of poetry is bound to have a strong subjective element in it and that is the source of the violent differences we find in the appreciation of any given author by equally "eminent" critics. All is relative here. Art and Beauty also, and our view of things and our appreciation of them depends on the consciousness which views and appreciates. Some critics recognise this and go in frankly for a purely subjective criticism — "this is why I like this and disapprove of that, I give my own values". Most however want to fit their personal likes and dislikes to some standard of criticism which they conceive to be objective; this need of objectivity, of the support of some impersonal truth independent of our personality, is the main source of theories, canons, standards of art. But the theories, canons, standards themselves vary and are set up in one age only to be broken in another.

> *Does this mean that there is no objective beauty of art independent of the differing temperaments of the observer? Is our experience of beauty a construction or a creation of our minds without having any objective existence otherwise?*

In that case Beauty is non-existent in Nature, it is put upon Nature by our minds through *adhyāropa*. But this contradicts the fact that it is in response to an object and not independently of it that the idea of beautiful or not beautiful originally rises within us. Beauty does exist in what we see, but there are two aspects of it, essential beauty and the form it takes. "Eternal beauty wandering on her way" does that wandering by a multitudinous variation of forms appealing to a multitudinous variation of consciousness. Therein comes the difficulty. Each individual consciousness tries to seize the eternal beauty expressed in a form (a particular poem or work of art), but is either drawn by the form or repelled by it, wholly attracted or wholly repelled, or partially attracted and partially repelled. There may be errors in the poet's or artist's transcription of beauty which mar the reception, but even these have different effects on different people. But the more radical divergences arise from the variation in the constitution of the mind and its difference of response.

But is it not possible for a catholic critic of art to overcome these limitations?

A critic cannot escape altogether from these limitations. He can try to make himself catholic and objective and find the merit or special character of all he reads or sees in poetry and art, even when they do not evoke his strongest sympathy or deepest response. I have little temperamental sympathy for much of the work of Pope and Dryden, but I can see their extraordinary perfection or force in their own field, the masterly conciseness, energy, point, metallic precision into which they cut their thought or their verse, and I can see too how that can with a little infusion of another quality be the basis of a really great poetic style, as Dryden himself has shown in his best work. But there my appreciation stops; I cannot rise to the heights of admiration of those who put them on a level with or on a higher level than Wordsworth, Keats or Shelley — I cannot escape from the feeling that their work, even though more consistently perfect within their limits and in their own manner (at least Pope's), was less great in poetic quality. These divergences rise from a conception of beauty and a feeling for beauty which belongs to the temperament. So too Housman's exaltation of Blake results directly from his feeling and peculiar conception of poetic beauty as an appeal to an inner sensation, an appeal marred and a beauty deflowered by bringing in a sharp coating or content of intellectual thought.

Does this mean that a critic cannot render any real help to others in the appreciation of beauty?

The critic can help to open the mind to the kinds of beauty he himself sees and not only to discover but to appreciate at their full value certain elements that make them beautiful or give them what is most characteristic or unique in their peculiar beauty. Housman, for instance, may help many minds to see in Blake something which they did not see before. They may not agree with him in his comparison of Blake and Shakespeare, but they can follow him to a certain extent and seize better that element in poetic beauty which he overstresses but makes at the same time more vividly visible.

X

INFLUENCE OF TRADITION AND ENVIRONMENT ON POETIC CREATION

To what extent is the work of a poet or an artist determined by the culture and the traditions of the nation to which he belongs?

The work of the poet depends not only on himself and his age, but on the mentality of the nation to which he belongs and the spiritual, intellectual, aesthetic tradition and environment which it creates for him. It is not to be understood by this that he is or need be entirely limited by this condition or that he is to consider himself as only a voice of the national mind or bound by the past national tradition and debarred from striking out a road of his own. In nations returning under difficulties to a strong self-consciousness, like the Irish or the Indian some time back, this nationalism may be a living idea and a powerful motive. And in others which have had a vivid collective life exercising a common and intimate influence on all their individuals or in those which have cherished an acute sense of a great national culture and tradition, the more stable elements of that tradition may exert a very conscious influence on the mind of the poets, at once helping and limiting the weaker spirits, but giving to genius an exceptional power for sustained beauty of form and a satisfying perfection. But this is no essential condition for the birth of great poetry. The poet, we must always remember, creates out of himself and has the indefeasible right to follow freely the breath of the spirit within him, provided he satisfies in his work the law of poetic beauty. The external forms of his age and his nation only give him his starting-point and some of his materials and determine to some extent the room he finds for the free play of his poetic spirit.

Generally, every nation or people has or develops a spirit in its being, a special soul-form of the human all-soul and a law of its nature which determines the lines and turns of its evolution. All that it takes from its environment it naturally attempts to assimilate to this spirit, transmute into stuff of his soul-form, make apt to and governable by this law of its nature. All its self-expression is in conformity with them. And its poetry, art and thought are the expression of this self and of the greater possibilities of its self to which it moves. The individual poet and his poetry are part of its movement. Not that they are limited by the present temperament and outward forms of the national mind; they may exceed them. The soul of the poet may be like a star and dwell apart; even, his work may seem not merely a variation from but a revolt against the limitations of the national mind. But still the roots of his personality are there in its spirit and even his variation and revolt are an attempt to bring out something that is latent and suppressed or at least something which is trying to surge up from the secret all-soul into the soul-form of the nation.

The historical school of literary criticism maintains that a poet's work is the product of his past and present circumstances and influences and that it is impossible to have a proper appreciation of his work without a study of these circumstances and influences. Is this true?

One cannot subscribe to this dogma of the historical school of criticism which asks of us to study all the precedents, circumstances, influences, surroundings, all that created the man and his work, — as if there were not something in him apart from all these which made all the difference, — and supposes that out of this the right estimate of his poetry will arise. But not even the right historical or psychological understanding of him need arise out of this method, since we may very easily read into him and his work things which may perhaps have been there before and around him, but never really got into him. But the right poetical estimate we certainly shall not form if we bring in so much that is accidental and unessential to cloud our free and direct impression. Rather the very opposite is the true method of appreciation, to come straight to the poet and his poem for all we need essentially to know about them, — we shall get there all that we really want for any true aesthetic or poetic purpose, — and afterwards go elsewhere for any minor elucidation or else to satisfy our scientific and historical curiosity; things accidental are then much more likely to fall into their right place and the freshness of poetic appreciation to remain unobscured. But quite apart from its external and therefore unreal method, there is a truth in the historical theory of criticism which is of real help towards grasping something that is important and even essential, if not for our poetic appreciation, yet for our intellectual judgment of a poet and his work.

What is the essential factor by which we should determine our response or appreciation of an artist's or a poet's work?

In poetry, as in everything else that aims at perfection, there are always two elements, the eternal and the time element. The first is what really and always matters, it is that which must determine our definitive appreciation, our absolute verdict, or rather our essential response to poetry. A soul expressing the eternal spirit of Truth and Beauty through some of the infinite variations of beauty, with the word for its instrument, that is, after all, what the poet is, and it is to a similar soul in us seeking the same spirit and responding to it that he makes his appeal. It is when we can get this response at its purest and in its most direct and heightened awakening that our faculty of poetic appreciation becomes at once surest and most intense. It is, we may say, the impersonal enjoyer of creative beauty in us responding to the impersonal creator and interpreter of beauty in the poet; for it is the impersonal spirit of Truth and Beauty that is seeking to express itself through his personality, and it is that which finds its own word and seems itself to create in his highest moments of inspiration. And this Impersonal is concerned with the creative idea and the motive of beauty which is seeking expression and with the attempt to find the perfect expression, the inevitable word and the rhythm that reveals. All else is subordinate, accidental, the crude material and the conditioning medium of this essential endeavour.

What then is the relative importance of the time element, which often considerably moulds a poet's personality, in evaluating his work?

There is also the personality of the poet and the personality of the hearer, the one giving the pitch and the form of the success arrived at, while the other determines the characteristic intellectual and aesthetic judgment to which its appeal arrives. The correspondence or the dissonance between the two decides the relation between the poet and his reader, and out of that arises what is personal in our appreciation and judgment of his poetry. In this personal or time element there is always much that is merely accidental and often rather limits and deflects our judgment than helps usefully to form it. How much that interferes can be seen when we try to value contemporary poetry. It is a matter of continual experience that even critics of considerable insight and sureness of taste are yet capable of the most extraordinarily wrong judgments, whether on the side of appreciation or of deprecation, when they have to pass a verdict on their contemporaries. And this is because a crowd of accidental influences belonging to the effect of the time and the mental environment upon our mentality exercise an exaggerated domination and distort or colour the view of our mental eyes upon its object.

Is the personal element then only a hindrance in our appreciation of poetry and art? Is there nothing essential in our present personality which has a right to be heard in this field?

We are all of us souls developing in a constant endeavour to get into unity with the spirit in life through its many forms of manifestation and on many different lines. And as there is in Indian Yoga a principle of *adhikāra*, something in the immediate power of a man's nature that determines by its characteristics his right to this or that way of Yoga, of union, which, whatever its merits or its limitations, is his right way because it is most helpful to him personally, so in all our activities of life and mind there is this principle of *adhikāra*. That which we can appreciate in poetry and still more the way in which we appreciate it, is that in it and us which is most helpful to us and therefore, for the time being at least, right for us in our attempt to get into union with the universal or the transcendent beauty through the revealing ideas and motives and revealing forms of poetic creation.

This is the individual aspect of the personal or time element. But there is also a larger movement to which we belong, both ourselves and the poet and his poetry; or rather it is the same movement of the general soul of mankind in the same endeavour towards the same objective. In poetry this shows itself in a sort of evolution from the objective to the inward, from the inward to the spiritual, an evolution which has many curves and turns and cycles, many returns upon past motives and imperfect anticipations of future motives, a general labour of self-enlargement and self-finding. It is a clear idea of this evoluton which may most helpfully inform the historical or evolutionary element in our judgment and appreciation of poetry.

XI

WESTERN MISUNDERSTANDING OF INDIAN ART

Most Europeans till very recently either completely failed to understand and appreciate the ancient Indian art or found it fantastic, ugly and repulsive. What is the root cause of this incomprehension?

The mental outlook of the European and the dislike of Indian art which it generates are rooted in something deeper than themselves, a whole cultural training, natural or acquired temperament and fundamental attitude towards existence, and it tries to measure the width of the gulf which till recently separated the oriental and the western mind and most of all the European and the Indian way of seeing things. An inability to understand the motives and methods of Indian art and contempt of or repulsion from it was almost universal till yesterday in the mind of Europe. There was little difference in this regard between the average man bound by his customary first notions and the competent critic trained to appreciate different forms of culture. The gulf was too wide for any bridge of culture then built to span. To the European mind Indian art was a thing barbarous, immature, monstrous, an arrested growth from humanity's primitive savagery and incompetent childhood. If there has been now some change, it is due to the remarkably sudden widening of the horizon and view of European culture, a partial shifting even of the standpoint from which it was accustomed to see and judge all that it saw. In matters of art the western mind was long bound up as in a prison in the Greek and Renaissance tradition modified by a later mentality with only two siderooms of escape, the romantic and the realistic motives, but these were only wings of the same building; for the base was the same and a common essential canon united their variations. The conventional superstition of the imitation of Nature as the first law or the limiting rule of art governed even the freest work and gave its tone to the artistic and critical intelligence. The canons of western artistic creation were held to be the sole valid criteria and everything else was regarded as primitive and half-developed or else strange and fantastic and interesting only by its curiosity.

Place this western mind before anything ancient, Hindu, Buddhistic or Vedantic in art and it looks at it with a blank or an angry incomprehension. It looks for the sense and does not find any, because either it has not in itself the experience and finds it difficult to have the imagination, much more the realisation of what this art does really mean and express, or because it insists on looking for what it is accustomed to see at home and, not finding that, is convinced that there is nothing to see or nothing of any value. Or else if there is something which it could have understood, it does not understand because it is expressed in the Indian form and the Indian way. It looks at the method and form and finds it unfamiliar, contrary to its own canons, is revolted, contemptuous, repelled, speaks of the thing as monstrous, barbarous, ugly or null, passes on in a high dislike or disdain. Or if it is overborne by some sense of unanalysable beauty of greatness or power it still speaks of a splendid barbarism. There we have the total incomprehension, the blind window, the blocked door in the mind, and there too the reason why the natural western mentality comes to Indian art with a demand for something other than what its characteristic spirit and motive intend to give, and, demanding that, is not prepared to enter into another kind of spiritual experience and another range of creative sight, imaginative power and mode of self-expression.

What is the fundamental difference in the spirit and method of Indian and European art which makes them so dissimilar?

All great artistic work proceeds from an act of intuition, not really an intellectual idea or a splendid imagination, — these are only mental translations, — but a direct intuition of some truth of life or being, some significant form of that truth, some development of it in the mind of man. And so far there is no difference between great European and great Indian work. Where then begins the immense divergence? It is there in everything else, in the object and field of the intuitive vision, in the method of working out the sight or suggestion, in the part taken in the rendering by the external form and technique, in the whole way of the rendering to the human mind, even in the centre of our being to which the work appeals. The European artist gets his intuition by a suggestion from an appearance in life and Nature or, if it starts from something in his own soul, relates it at once to an external support. He brings down that intuition into his normal mind and sets the intellectual idea and the imagination in the intelligence to clothe it with a mental stuff which will render its form to the moved reason, emotion, aesthesis. Then he missions his eye and hand to execute it in terms which start from a colourable "imitation" of life and nature — and in ordinary hands too often end there — to get at an interpretation that really changes it into the image of something not outward in our own being or in universal being which was the real thing seen. And to that in looking at the work we have to get back through colour and line and disposition or whatever else may be part of the external means, to their mental suggestions and through them to the soul of the whole matter. The appeal is not direct to the eye of the deepest self and spirit within, but to the outward soul by a strong awakening of the sensuous, the vital, the emotional, the intellectual and imaginative being, and of the spiritual we get as much or as little as can suit itself to and express itself through the outward man. Life, action, passion, emotion, idea, Nature seen for their own sake and for an aesthetic delight in them, these are the object and field of this creative intuition. The something more which the Indian mind knows to be behind these things looks out, if at all, from behind many veils. The direct and unveiled presence of the Infinite and its godheads is not evoked or thought necessary to the greater greatness and the highest perfection.

How do the central aim and governing principle of ancient

Indian art differ from those of European art?

The theory of ancient Indian art at its greatest — and the greatest gives its character to the rest and throws on it something of its stamp and influence — is of another kind. Its highest business is to disclose something of the Self, the Infinite, the Divine to the regard of the soul, the Self through its expressions, the Infinite through its living finite symbols, the Divine through his powers. Or the Godheads are to be revealed, luminously interpreted or in some way suggested to the soul's understanding or to its devotion or at the very least to a spiritually or religiously aesthetic emotion. When this hieratic art comes down from these altitudes to the intermediate worlds behind ours, to the lesser godheads or genii, it still carries into them some power or some hint from above. And when it comes quite down to the material world and the life of man and the things of external Nature, it does not altogether get rid of the greater vision, the hieratic stamp, the spiritual seeing, and in most good work — except in moments of relaxation and a humorous or vivid play with the obvious — there is always something more in which the seeing presentation of life floats as in an immaterial atmosphere. Life is seen in the self or in some suggestion of the infinite or of something beyond or there is at least a touch and influence of these which helps to shape the presentation.

Can we say that all the works of ancient Indian art fulfil this high aim?

It is not that all Indian work realises this ideal, there is plenty no doubt that falls short, is lowered, ineffective or even debased, but it is the best and the most characteristic influence and execution which gives its tone to an art and by which we must judge.

What is the main difference between the European and the Indian artist's treatment of form?

A seeing in the self is the characteristic method of the Indian artist and it is directly enjoined on him by the canon. He has to see first in his spiritual being the truth of the thing he must express and to create its form in his intuitive mind; he is not bound to look out first on outward life and Nature for his model, his authority, his rule, his teacher or his fountain of suggestions. Why should he when it is something quite inward he has to bring out into expression? It is not an idea in the intellect, a mental imagination, an outward emotion on which he has to depend for his stimulants, but an idea, image, emotion of the spirit, and the mental equivalents are subordinate things for help in the transmission and give only a part of the colouring and the shape. A material form, colour, line and design are his physical means of the expression, but in using them he is not bound to an imitation of Nature, but has to make the form and all else significant of his vision, and if that can only be done or can best be done by some modification, some pose, some touch or symbolic variation which is not found in physical Nature, he is at perfect liberty to use it, since truth to his vision, the unity of the thing he is seeing and expressing is his only business. The line, colour and the rest are not his first, but his last preoccupation, because they have to carry on them a world of things which have already taken spiritual form in his mind. He has not for instance to re-create for us the human face and body of the Buddha or some one passion or incident of his life, but to reveal the calm of Nirvana through a figure of the Buddha, and every detail and accessory must be turned into a means or an aid of his purpose. And even when it is some human passion or incident he has to portray, it is not usually that alone, but also or more something else in the soul to which it points or from which it starts or some power behind the action that has to enter into the spirit of his design and is often really the main thing. And through the eye that looks on his work he has to appeal not merely to an excitement of the outward soul, but to the inner self, *antarātman*. One may well say that beyond the ordinary cultivation of the aesthetic instinct necessary to all artistic appreciation there is a spiritual insight or culture needed if we are to enter into the whole meaning of Indian artistic creation, otherwise we get only at the surface of external things or at the most at things only just below the surface. It is an intuitive and spiritual art and must be seen with the intuitive and spiritual eye.

What was the relation between the pursuit of art and other cultural and higher pursuits like those of philosophy, religion and Yoga in ancient India?

Indian art in fact is identical in its spiritual aim and principle with the rest of Indian culture. Indian architecture, painting, sculpture are not only intimately one in inspiration with the central things in Indian philosophy, religion, Yoga, culture, but a specially intense expression of their significance. There is much in the literature which can be well enough appreciated without any very deep entry into these things, but it is comparatively a very small part of what is left of the other arts, Hindu or Buddhistic, of which this can be said. They have been very largely a hieratic aesthetic script of India's spiritual, contemplative and religious experience.

XII

ANCIENT INDIAN ARCHITECTURE (1)

What is the right way of looking at Indian works of art which the western mind generally misses, thus failing to arrive at their true import and significance?

The characteristic attitude of the Indian reflective and creative mind necessitates in our view of its creations an effort to get beyond at once to the inner spirit of the reality it expresses and see from it and not from outside. And in fact to start from the physical details and their synthesis appears to me quite the wrong way to look at an Indian work of art. The orthodox style of western criticism seems to be to dwell scrutinisingly on the technique, on form, on the obvious story of the form, and then pass to some appreciation of beautiful or impressive emotion and idea. It is only in some deeper and more sensitive minds that we get beyond that depth into profounder things. A criticism of that kind applied to Indian art leaves it barren or poor of significance. Here the only right way is to get at once through a total intuitive or revelatory impression or by some meditative dwelling on the whole, *dhyāna* in the technical Indian term, to the spiritual meaning and atmosphere, make ourselves one with that as completely as possible, and then only the helpful meaning and value of all the rest comes out with a complete and revealing force. For here it is the spirit that carries the form, while in most western art it is the form that carries whatever there may be of spirit. The striking phrase of Epictetus recurs to the mind in which he describes man as a little soul carrying a corpse, *psucharion ei bastazon nekron*. The more ordinary western outlook is upon animate matter carrying in its life a modicum of soul. But the seeing of the Indian mind and of Indian art is that of a great, a limitless self and spirit, *mahān ātmā*, which carries to us in the sea of its presence a living shape of itself, small in comparison to its own infinity, but yet sufficient by the power that informs this symbol to support some aspect of that infinite's self-expression. It is therefore essential that we should look here not solely with the physical eye informed by the reason and the aesthetic imagination, but make the physical seeing a passage to the opening of the inner spiritual eye and a moved communion in the soul. A great oriental work of art does not easily reveal its secret to one who comes to it solely in a mood of aesthetic curiosity or with a considering critical objective mind, still less as the cultivated and interested tourist passing among strange and foreign things; but it has to be seen in loneliness, in the solitude of one's self, in moments when one is capable of long and deep meditation and as little weighted as possible with the conventions of material life. That is why the Japanese with their fine sense in these things, — a sense which modern Europe with her assault of crowded art galleries and over-pictured walls seems to have quite lost, though perhaps I am wrong, and those are the right conditions for display of European art, — have put their temples and their Buddhas as often as possible away on mountains and in distant or secluded scenes of Nature and avoid living with great paintings in the crude hours of daily life, but keep them by preference in such a way that their undisputed suggestion can sink into the mind in its finer moments or apart where they can go and look at them in a treasured secrecy when the soul is at leisure from life. That is an indication of the utmost value pointing to the nature of the appeal made by eastern art and the right way and mood for looking at its creations.

Is this way of approach necessary for a proper appreciation of ancient Indian architecture?

Indian architecture especially demands this kind of inner study and this spiritual self-identification with its deepest meaning and will not otherwise reveal itself to us. These sacred buildings are the signs, the architectural self-expression of an ancient spiritual and religious culture. Ignore the spiritual suggestion, the religious significance, the meaning of the symbols and indications, look only with the rational and secular aesthetic mind, and it is vain to expect that we shall get to any true and discerning appreciation of this art. And it has to be remembered too that the religious spirit here is something quite different from the sense of European religions; and even mediaeval Christianity, especially as now looked at by the modern European mind which has gone through the two great crises of the Renascence and recent secularism, will not in spite of its oriental origin and affinities be of much real help. To bring in into the artistic look on an Indian temple occidental memories or a comparison with the Greek Parthenon or Italian church or Duomo or Campanile or even the great Gothic cathedrals of mediaeval France, though these have in them something much nearer to the Indian mentality, is to intrude a fatally foreign and disturbing element or standard in the mind. But this consciously or else subconsciously is what almost every European mind does to a greater or less degree, — and it is here a pernicious immixture, for it subjects the work of a vision that saw the immeasurable to the tests of an eye that dwells only on measure.

Some European art critics have remarked that Indian architecture lacks in unity which is a fundamental requirement of all art. Is this true?

The failure to see at once the unity of this architecture is perfectly natural to a European eye, because unity in the sense demanded by the western conception, the Greek unity gained by much suppression and a sparing use of detail and circumstance or even the Gothic unity got by casting everything into the mould of a single spiritual aspiration, is not there. And the greater unity that really is there can never be arrived at at all, if the eye begins and ends by dwelling on form and detail and ornament, because it will then be obsessed by these things and find it difficult to go beyond to the unity which all this in its totality serves not so much to express in itself, but to fill it with that which comes out of it and relieve its oneness by multitude. An original oneness, not a combined or synthetic or an effected unity, is that from which this art begins and to which its work when finished returns or rather lives in it as in its self and natural atmosphere. Indian sacred architecture constantly represents the greatest oneness of the Self, the cosmic, the infinite in the immensity of its world-design, the multitude of its features of self-expression, *lakṣaṇa,* (yet the oneness is greater than and independent of their totality and in itself indefinable), and all its starting-point of unity in conception, its mass of design and immensity of material, its crowding abundance of significant ornament and detail and its return towards oneness are only intelligible as necessary circumstances of this poem, this epic or this lyric — for there are smaller structures which are such lyrics — of the Infinite. The western mentality, except in those who are coming or returning, since Europe had once something of this cult in her own way, to this vision, may find it difficult to appreciate the truth and meaning of such an art, which tries to figure existence as a whole and not in its pieces; but I would invite those Indian minds who are troubled by these criticisms or partly or temporarily overpowered by the western way of seeing things, to look at our architecture in the light of this conception and see whether all but minor objections do not vanish as soon as the real meaning makes itself felt and gives body to the first indefinable impression and emotion which we experience before the greater constructions of the Indian builders.

The objection of lack of unity in Indian architecture is derived partly from the fact that it teems with an excessive crowding of ornamental detail which the western critic finds very confusing and distasteful. How far is this objection sound?

The objection that an excess of thronging detail and ornament hides, impairs or breaks up the unity, is advanced only because the eye has made the mistake of dwelling on the detail first without relation to this original spiritual openness, which has first to be fixed in an intimate spiritual seeing and union and then all else seen in that vision and experience. When we look on the multiplicity of the world, it is only a crowded plurality that we can find and to arrive at unity we have to reduce, to suppress what we have seen or sparingly select a few indications or to be satisfied with the unity of this or that separate idea, experience or imagination; but when we have realised the Self, the infinite unity, and look back on the multiplicity of the world, then we find that oneness which is able to bear all the infinity of variation and circumstance we can crowd into it and its unity remains unabridged by even the most endless self-multiplication of its informing creation. We find the same thing in looking at this architecture. The wealth of ornament, detail, circumstance in Indian temples represents the infinite variety and repetition of the worlds, — not our world only, but all the planes, — suggests the infinite multiplicity in the infinite oneness. It is a matter of our own experience and fullness of vision how much we leave out or bring in, whether we express so much or so little or attempt as in the Dravidian style to give the impression of a teeming inexhaustible plenitude. The largeness of this unity is base and continent enough for any super-structure or content of multitude.

To condemn this abundance as barbarous is to apply a foreign standard. Where after all are we bound to draw the line? To the pure classical taste Shakespeare's art once appeared great but barbarous for a similar reason, — one remembers the Gallic description of him as a drunken barbarian of genius, — his artistic unity non-existent or spoilt by crowding tropical vegetation of incident and character, his teeming imaginations violent, exaggerated, sometimes bizarre, monstrous, without symmetry, proportion and all the other lucid unities, lightnesses, graces loved by the classic mind. That mind might say of his work that here there is indeed a titanic genius, a mass of power, but of unity, clarity, classic nobility no trace, but rather an entire absence of lucid grace and lightness and restraint, a profusion of wild ornament and an imaginative riot without law or measure, strained figures, distorted positions and gestures, no dignity, no fine, just, rationally natural and beautiful classic movement and pose. But even the strictest Latin mind has now got over its objections to the "splendid barbarism" of Shakespeare and can understand that here is a fuller, less sparing and exiguous vision of life, a greater intuitive unity than the formal unities of the classic aesthesis. But the Indian vision of the world and existence was vaster and fuller than Shakespeare's, because it embraced not merely life, but all being, not merely humanity, but all the worlds and all Nature and cosmos. The European mind not having arrived except in individuals at any close, direct, insistent realisation of the unity of the infinite Self or the cosmic consciousness peopled with its infinite multiplicity, is not driven to express these things, cannot understand or put up with them when they are expressed in this oriental art, speech and style and object to it as the Latin mind once objected to Shakespeare. Perhaps the day is not distant when it will see and understand and perhaps even itself try to express the same things in another language.

XIII

ANCIENT INDIAN ARCHITECTURE (2)

Some European critics also object to the overloading of details in Indian architecture on the ground that it leaves no unfilled spaces to provide the necessary relief to the eye. Is there any truth in this objection?

The objection that the crowding detail allows no calm, gives no relief or space to the eye, falls under the same heading, springs from the same root, is urged from a different experience and has no validity for the Indian experience. For this unity on which all is upborne, carries in itself the infinite space and calm of the spiritual realisation, and there is no need for other unfilled spaces or tracts of calm of a lesser more superficial kind. The eye is here only a way of access to the soul, it is to that that there is the appeal, and if the soul living in this realisation or dwelling under the influence of this aesthetic impression needs any relief, it is not from the incidence of life and form, but from the immense incidence of that vastness of infinity and tranquil silence, and that can only be given by its opposite, by an abundance of form and detail and life.

Some European critics feel oppressed by the massive and often stupendous constructions of Dravidian architecture in South India and find in them a complete lack of grace and beauty. Is this impression quite valid?

As for the objection in regard to Dravidian architecture to its massiveness and its titanic construction, the precise spiritual effect intended could not be given otherwise; for the infinite, the cosmic seen as a whole in its vast manifestation is titanic, is mighty in material and power. It is other and quite different things also, but none of these are absent from Indian construction. The great temples of the north have often a singular grace in their power, a luminous lightness relieving their mass and strength, a rich delicacy of beauty in their ornate fullness. It is not indeed the Greek lightness, clarity or naked nobleness, nor is it exclusive, but comes in in a fine blending of opposites which is in the very spirit of the Indian religious, philosophical and aesthetic mind. Nor are these things absent from many Dravidian buildings, though in certain styles they are boldly sacrificed or only put into minor incidents, but in either case suppressed so that the fullness of solemn and grandiose effect may have a complete, an undiminished expression.

Many Europeans feel a sense of monstrous terror and gloom in the mighty constructions of Indian architecture. What is the reason for this?

Even a sympathetic mind like Professor Geddes is impressed by some sense of a monstrous effect of terror and gloom in these mighty buildings. Such expressions are astonishing to an Indian mind because terror and gloom are conspicuously absent from the feelings aroused in it by its religion, art or literature. In the religion they are rarely awakened and only in order to be immediately healed and, even when they come, are always sustained by the sense of a supporting and helping presence, an eternal greatness and calm or love or Delight behind; the very goddess of destruction is at the same time the compassionate and loving Mother; the austere Maheswara, Rudra, is also Shiva, the auspicious, Asutosha, the refuge of men. The Indian thinking and religious mind looks with calm, without shrinking or repulsion, with an understanding born of its agelong effort at identity and oneness, at all that meets it in the stupendous spectacle of the cosmos. And even its asceticism, its turning from the world, which begins not in terror and gloom, but in a sense of vanity and fatigue, or of something higher, truer, happier than life, soon passes beyond any element of pessimistic sadness into the rapture of the eternal peace and bliss. Indian secular poetry and drama is throughout rich, vital and joyous and there is more tragedy, terror, sorrow, and gloom packed into any few pages of European work than we can find in the whole mass of Indian literature. It does not seem to me that Indian art is at all different in this respect from the religion and literature. The western mind is here thrusting in its own habitual reactions upon things in the indigenous conception in which they have no proper place. Mark the curious misreading of the dance of Shiva as a dance of Death or Destruction, whereas, as anybody ought to be able to see who looks upon the Nataraja, it expresses on the contrary the rapture of the cosmic dance with the profundities behind of the unmoved eternal and infinite bliss. So too the figure of Kali which is so terrible to European eyes is, as we know, the Mother of the universe accepting this fierce aspect of destruction in order to slay the Asuras, the powers of evil in man and the world. There are other strands in this feeling in the western mind which seem to spring from a dislike of anything uplifted far beyond the human measure and others again in which we see a subtle survival of the Greek limitation, the fear, gloom and aversion with which the sunny terrestrial Hellenic mind commonly met the idea of the beyond, the limitless, the unknown; but that reaction has no place in Indian mentality. And as for the strangeness or formidable aspect of certain unhuman figures or the conception of demons or rakshasas, it must be remembered that the Indian aesthetic mind deals not only with the earth but with psychic planes in which these things exist and ranges freely among them without being overpowered because it carries everywhere the stamp of a large confidence in the strength and the omnipresence of the Self or the Divine.

In the exquisite and magical beauty of the Indo-Moslem architecture of Northern India some western critics have found an expression of the unbridled sensuous luxury and effeminate decadence of the time. Is there any validity in this view?

Is it true that there is nothing but a sensuous outward grace and beauty and luxury in these Indo-Moslem buildings? It is not at all true of the characteristic greater work. The Taj is not merely a sensuous reminiscence of an imperial amour or a fairy enchantment hewn from the moon's lucent quarries, but the eternal dream of a love that survives death. The great mosques embody often a religious aspiration lifted to a noble austerity which supports and is not lessened by the subordinated ornament and grace. The tombs reach beyond death to the beauty and joy of Paradise. The buildings of Fatehpur-Sikri are not monuments of an effeminate luxurious decadence, — an absurd description of the mind of the time of Akbar, — but give form to a nobility, power and beauty which lay hold upon but do not wallow on the earth. There is not here indeed the vast spiritual content of the earlier Indian mind, but it is still an Indian mind which in these delicate creations absorbs the West Asian influence, and lays stress on the sensuous as before in the poetry of Kalidasa, but uplifts it to a certain immaterial charm, rises often from the earth without quite leaving it into the magical beauty of the middle world and in the religious mood touches with a devout hand the skirts of the Divine. The all-pervading spiritual obsession is not there, but other elements of life not ignored by Indian culture and gaining on it since the classical times are here brought out under a new influence and are still penetrated with some radiant glow of a superior lustre.

There has been a tendency among western critics to attribute a foreign origin to whatever survives of ancient Indian art. Numerous attempts have been made by these critics to ascribe the Ajanta paintings to the Greeks, Persians or Chinese and it is even maintained that the Kangara paintings are of European inspiration and were painted for the English market. So also the sculptures of Gandhara are said to be Greek in origin and the Tajmahal to be the work of an Italian sculptor. Is there any truth in the contention?

The plain fact is that whatever outside influences there may or may not have been in India as elsewhere, even the earliest work shows a characteristic Indian mentality and touch; and as for

Gandharan art, it has the air of an inefficient attempt of the Hellenistic mind to absorb this spirit rather than an effort of India to imitate Greece. And in any case the great characteristic work could no more have been the creation of a foreign mind or of its influence than the sculptures of Phidias can be attributed to an Assyrian, Egyptian or Chinese origin. A psychological insensibility to the spiritual significance of Indian work is probably at the root of these errors and, so long as that subsists, the most erudite knowledge will be no protection against gross misunderstandings.[1]

---

1. The attitude and regard of the cultured European mind on Indian and Eastern art has immensely changed since this was written and there has been a great progress towards sympathy and understanding and even developments due to an oriental influence. There is indeed some survival of old prejudices but this is no longer the characteristic standpoint of the aesthetic mind of Europe towards the creative achievement of India or of Asia. (Sri Aurobindo's note.)

XIV

ANCIENT INDIAN SCULPTURE

Why did the art of sculpture flourish greatly only in ancient times in countries like Egypt, Greece and India, while in mediaeval and modern Europe it was in the art of painting that rich and abundant work was produced?

The difference arises from the different kind of mentality required by the two arts. The material in which we work makes its own peculiar demand on the creative spirit, lays down its own natural conditions, as Ruskin has pointed out in a different connection, and the art of making in stone or bronze calls for a cast of mind which the ancients had and the moderns have not or have had only in rare individuals, an artistic mind not too rapidly mobile and self-indulgent, not too much mastered by its own personality and emotion and the touches that excite and pass, but founded rather on some great basis of assured thought and vision, stable in temperament, fixed in its imagination on things that are firm and enduring. One cannot trifle with ease in this sterner material, one cannot even for long or with safety indulge in them in mere grace and external beauty or the more superficial, mobile and lightly attractive motives. The aesthetic self-indulgence which the soul of colour permits and even invites, the attraction of the mobile play of life to which line of brush, pen or pencil gives latitude, are here forbidden or, if to some extent achieved, only within a line of restraint to cross which is perilous and soon fatal. Here grand or profound motives are called for, a more or less penetrating spiritual vision or some sense of things eternal to base the creation. The sculptural art is static, self-contained, necessarily firm, noble or severe and demands an aesthetic spirit capable of these qualities. A certain mobility of life and mastering grace of line can come in upon this basis, but if it entirely replaces the original Dharma of the material, that means that the spirit of the statuette has come into the statue and we may be sure of an approaching decadence. Hellenic sculpture following this line passed from the greatness of Phidias through the soft self-indulgence of Praxiteles to its decline. A later Europe has failed for the most part in sculpture, in spite of some great work by individuals, an Angelo or a Rodin, because it played externally with stone and bronze, took them as a medium for the representation of life and could not find a sufficient basis of profound vision or spiritual motive. In Egypt and in India, on the contrary, sculpture preserved its power of successful creation through several great ages. The earliest work recently discovered in India dates back to the fifth century B.C. and is already fully evolved with an evident history of consummate previous creation behind it, and the latest work of some high value comes down to within a few centuries from our own time. An assured history of two millenniums of accomplished sculptural creation is a rare and significant fact in the life of a people.

What is the cause of this greatness and continuity of Indian sculpture?

This greatness and continuity of Indian sculpture is due to the close connection between the religious and philosophical and the aesthetic mind of the people. Its survival into times not far from us was possible because of the survival of the cast of the antique mind in that philosophy and religion, a mind familiar with eternal things, capable of cosmic vision, having its roots of thought and seeing in the profundities of the soul, in the most intimate pregnant and abiding experiences of the human spirit. The more ancient sculptural art of India embodies in visible form what the Upanishads threw out into inspired thought and the Mahabharata and Ramayana portrayed by the word. This sculpture like the architecture springs from spiritual realisation, and what it creates and expresses at its greatest is the spirit in form, the soul in body, this or that living soul-power in the divine or the human, the universal and cosmic individualised in suggestion but not lost in individuality, the impersonal supporting a not too insistent play of personality, the abiding moments of the eternal, the presence, the idea, the power, the calm or potent delight of the spirit in its actions and creations. And over all the art something of this intention broods and persists and is suggested even where it does not dominate the mind of the sculptor. And therefore as in the architecture so in the sculpture, we have to bring a different mind to this work, a different capacity of vision and response, we have to go deeper into ourselves to see than in the more outwardly imaginative art of Europe.

What is the essential difference between the greatness of Greek and Indian sculpture?

The earlier and more archaic Greek style had indeed something in it which looks like a reminiscent touch of a first creative origin from Egypt and the Orient, but there is already there the governing conception which determined the Greek aesthesis and has dominated the later mind of Europe, the will to combine some kind of expression of an inner truth with an idealising imitation of external Nature. The brilliance, beauty and nobility of the work which was accomplished, was a very great and perfect thing, but it is idle to maintain that that is the sole possible method or the one permanent and natural law of artistic creation. Its highest greatness subsisted only so long — and it was not for very long — as a certain satisfying balance was struck and constantly maintained between a fine, but not very subtle, opulent or profound spiritual suggestion and an outward physical harmony of nobility and grace. A later work achieved a brief miracle of vital suggestion and sensuous physical grace with a certain power of expressing the spirit of beauty in the mould of the senses; but this once done, there was no more to see or create. For the curious turn which impels at the present day the modern mind to return to spiritual vision through a fiction of exaggerated realism which is really a pressure upon the form of things to yield the secret of the spirit in life and matter, was not open to the classic temperament and intelligence. And it is surely time for us to see, as is now by many admitted, that an acknowledgment of the greatness of Greek art in its own province ought not to prevent the plain perception of the rather strait and narrow bounds of that province. What Greek sculpture expressed was fine, gracious and noble, but what it did not express and could not by the limitations of its canon hope to attempt, was considerable, was immense in possibility, was that spiritual depth and extension which the human mind needs for its larger and deeper self-experience. And just this is the greatness of Indian sculpture that it expresses in stone and bronze what the Greek aesthetic mind could not conceive or express and embodies it with a profound understanding of its right conditions and a native perfection.

How is this difference of aesthetic conception reflected in the figures of gods and human beings created by the Greek and Indian sculptors?

The Olympian gods of Phidias are magnified and uplifted human beings saved from a too human limitation by a certain divine calm of impersonality or universalised quality, divine type, *guṇa*; in other work we see heroes, athletes, feminine incarnations of beauty, calm and restrained embodiments of idea, action or emotion in the idealised beauty of the human figure. The gods of Indian sculpture are cosmic beings, embodiments of some great spiritual power, spiritual idea and action, inmost psychic significance, the human form a vehicle of this soul meaning, its outward means of self-expression; everything in the figure, every opportunity it gives, the face, the hands, the posture of the limbs, the poise and turn of the body, every accessory, has to be made instinct with the inner meaning, help it to emerge, carry out the rhythm of the total suggestion, and on the other hand everything is suppressed which would defeat this end, especially all that would mean an insistence on the merely vital or physical, outward or obvious suggestions of the human figure. Not the ideal physical or emotional beauty, but the utmost spiritual beauty or significance of which the human form is capable, is the aim of this kind of creation. The divine self in us is its theme, the body made a form of the soul is its idea and its secret. And therefore in front of this art it is not enough to look at it and respond with the aesthetic eye and the imagination, but we must look also into the form for what it carries and even through and behind it to pursue the profound suggestion it gives into its own infinite. The religious or hieratic side of Indian sculpture is intimately connected with the spiritual experiences of Indian meditation and adoration, soul realisation is its method of creation and soul realisation must be the way of our response and understanding. And even with the figures of human beings or groups it is still a like inner aim and vision which governs the labour of the sculptor. The statue of a king or a saint is not meant merely to give the idea of a king or saint or to portray some dramatic action or to be a character portrait in stone, but to embody rather a soul-state or experience or deeper soul-quality, as for instance, not the outward emotion, but the inner soul-side of rapt ecstasy of adoration and God-vision in the saint or the devotee before the presence of the worshipped deity. This is the character of the task the Indian sculptor set before his effort and it is according to his success in that and not by the absence of something else, some quality or some intention foreign to his mind and contrary to his design, that we have to judge of his achievement and his labour.

What is the place of Indian sculpture amongst the sculptures of the world?

Each manner of art has its own ideals, traditions, agreed conventions; for the ideas and forms of the creative spirit are many, though there is one ultimate basis. The perspective, the psychic vision of the Chinese and Japanese painters are not the same as those of European artists; but who can ignore the beauty and the wonder of their work? The essence of the question lies in the rendering of the truth and beauty seized by the spirit.

Indian sculpture, Indian art in general follows its own ideal and traditions and these are unique in their character and quality. It is the expression, great as a whole through many centuries and ages of creation, supreme at its best, whether in rare early pre-Asokan, in Asokan or later work of the first heroic age or in the magnificent statues of the cave-cathedrals and Pallava and other southern temples or the noble, accomplished or gracious imagination of Bengal, Nepal and Java through the later centuries or in the singular skill and delicacy of the bronze work of the southern religions, a self-expression of the spirit and ideals of a great nation and a great culture which stands apart in the cast of its mind and qualities among the earth's peoples, famed for its spiritual achievement, its deep philosophies and its religious spirit, its artistic taste, the richness of its poetic imagination, and not inferior to any of the older civilisations in its dealings with life and its social endeavour and political institutions. This sculpture is a singularly powerful, a seizing and profound interpretation in stone and bronze of the inner soul of that people.

XV

ANCIENT INDIAN PAINTING

It has been maintained by some critics that, unlike the arts of architecture and sculpture, the art of painting in ancient and later India flourished only at intervals and had no continuous tradition. Is this true?

This is a hasty view that does not outlast a more careful research and consideration of the available evidence. It appears, on the contrary, that Indian culture was able to arrive at a well developed and an understanding aesthetic use of colour and line from very early times and, allowing for the successive fluctuations, periods of decline and fresh outbursts of originality and vigour, which the collective human mind undergoes in all countries, used this form of self-expression very persistently through the long centuries of its growth and greatness. And especially it is apparent now that there was a persistent tradition, a fundamental spirit and turn of the aesthetic sense native to the mind of India which links even the latest Rajput art to the earliest surviving work still preserved at its highest summit of achievement in the rock-cut retreats of Ajanta.

The materials of the art of painting are unfortunately more perishable than those of any other of the greater means of creative aesthetic self-expression and of the ancient masterpieces only a little survives but that little still indicates the immensity of the amount of work of which it is the fading remnant. It is said that of the twenty-nine caves at Ajanta almost all once bore signs of decoration by frescoes; only so long ago as forty years sixteen still contained something of the original paintings, but now six alone still bear their witness to the greatness of this ancient art, though rapidly perishing and deprived of something of the original warmth and beauty and glory of colour. The rest of all that vivid contemporaneous creation which must at one time have covered the whole country in the temples and *vihāras* and the houses of the cultured and the courts and pleasure-houses of nobles and kings, has perished, and we have only, more or less similar to the work at Ajanta, some crumbling fragments of rich and profuse decoration in the caves of Bagh and a few paintings of female figures in two rock-cut chambers at Sigiriya[1]. These remnants represent the work of some six or seven centuries, but they leave gaps, and nothing now remains of any paintings earlier than the first century of the Christian era, except some frescoes, spoilt by unskilful restoration, from the first century before it, while after the seventh there is a blank which might at first sight argue a total decline of the art, a cessation and disappearance. But there are fortunately evidences which carry back the tradition of the art at one end many centuries earlier and other remains more recently discovered and of another kind outside India and in the Himalayan countries which carry it forward at the other end as late as the twelfth century and help us to link it on to the later schools of Rajput painting. The history of the self-expression of the Indian mind in painting covers a period of as much as two millenniums of more or less intense artistic creation and stands on a par in this respect with the architecture and sculpture.

As the surviving ancient paintings are the work of Buddhist painters, it is maintained that in the pre-Buddhistic period the art of painting did not exist in India. Is this inference valid?

The paintings that remain to us from ancient times are the work of Buddhist painters, but the art itself in India was of pre-Buddhistic origin. The Tibetan historian ascribes a remote antiquity in all the crafts, prior to the Buddha, and this is a conclusion increasingly pointed to by a constant accumulation of evidence. Already in the third century before the Christian era, we find the theory of the art well founded from previous times, the six essential elements, *ṣaḍaṅga*, recognised and enu-

---

[1]. Since then more paintings of high quality have been found in some southern temples, akin in their spirit and style to the work at Ajanta. (Sri Aurobindo's note.)

merated, like the more or less corresponding six Chinese canons which are first mentioned nearly a thousand years later, and in a very ancient work on the art pointing back to pre-Buddhistic times a number of careful and very well-defined rules and traditions are laid down which were developed into an elaborate science of technique and traditional rule in the later *Shilpasutras*. The frequent references in the ancient literature also are of a character which would have been impossible without widespread practice and appreciation of the art by both men and women of the cultured classes, and these allusions and incidents evidencing a moved delight in the painted form and beauty of colour and the appeal both to the decorative sense and to the aesthetic emotion occur not only in the later poetry of Kalidasa, Bhavabhuti and other classical dramatists, but in the early popular drama of Bhasa and earlier still in the epics and in the sacred books of the Buddhists.

Some critics observe that the pre-Buddhistic Hindu painting of ancient India was purely secular in motive and inspiration and not religious or spiritual like the Buddhist painting. Is this view justifiable?

It is true that while the surviving work of Buddhist artists is mainly religious in subject or at least links on common scenes of life to Buddhist ceremony and legend, the references in the epic and dramatic literature are usually to painting of a more purely aesthetic character, personal, domestic or civic, portrait painting, the representation of scenes and incidents in the lives of kings and other great personalities or mural decoration of palaces and private or public buildings. On the other hand, there are similar elements in Buddhist painting, as, for example, the portraits of the queens of King Kashyapa at Sigiriya, the historic representation of a Persian embassy or the landing of Vijaya in Ceylon. And we may fairly assume that all along Indian painting both Buddhist and Hindu covered much the same kind of ground as the later Rajput work in a more ample fashion and with a more antique greatness of spirit and was in its ensemble an interpretation of the whole religion, culture and life of the Indian people. The one important and significant thing that emerges is the constant oneness and continuity of all Indian art in its essential spirit and tradition. Thus the earlier work at Ajanta has been found to be akin to the earlier sculptural work of the Buddhists, while the later paintings have a similar close kinship to the sculptural reliefs at Java. And we find that the spirit and tradition which reigns through all changes of style and manner at Ajanta, is present too at Bagh and Sigiriya, in the Khotan frescoes, in the illuminations of Buddhist manuscripts of a much later time and in spite of the change of form and manner is still spiritually the same in the Rajput paintings.

How does Indian painting differ from Indian sculpture in its essential spirit and aim?

The spirit and motive of Indian painting are in their centre of conception and shaping force of sight identical with the inspiring vision of Indian sculpture. All Indian art is a throwing out of a certain profound self-vision formed by a going within to find out the secret significance of form and appearance, a discovery of the subject in one's deeper self, the giving of soul-form to that vision and a remoulding of the material and natural shape to express the psychic truth of it with the greatest possible purity and power of outline and the greatest possible concentrated rhythmic unity of significance in all the parts of an indivisible artistic whole. Take whatever masterpiece of Indian painting and we shall find these conditions aimed at and brought out into a triumphant beauty of suggestion and execution. The only difference from the other arts comes from the turn natural and inevitable to its own kind of aesthesis, from the moved and indulgent dwelling on what one might call the mobilities of the soul rather than on its static eternities, on the casting out of self into grace and movement of psychic and vital life (subject always to the reserve and restraint necessary to all art) rather than on the holding back of life in the stabilities of the self and its eternal qualities and principles, *guṇa* and *tattva*. This distinction is of the very essence of the difference between the work given to the sculptor and the painter, a difference imposed on them by the natural scope, turn, possibility of their instrument, and medium. The sculptor must express always in static form; the idea of the spirit is cut out for him in mass and line, significant in the stability of its insistence, and he can lighten the weight of this insistence but not get rid of it or away from it; for him eternity seizes hold of time in its shapes and arrests it in the monumental spirit of stone or bronze. The painter on the contrary lavishes his soul in colour and there is a liquidity in the form, a fluent grace of subtlety in the line he uses which imposes on him a more mobile and emotional way of self-expression. The more he gives us of the colour and changing form and emotion of the life of the soul, the more his work glows with beauty, masters the inner aesthetic sense and opens it to the thing his art better gives us than any other, the delight of the motion of the self out into a spiritually sensuous joy of beautiful shapes and the coloured radiances of existence. Painting is naturally the most sensuous of the arts and the highest greatness open to the painter is to spiritualise this sensuous appeal by making the most vivid outward beauty a revelation of subtle spiritual emotion so that the soul and the sense are at harmony in the deepest and finest richness of both and united in their satisfied consonant expression of the inner significances of things and life. There is less of the austerity of *tapasyā* in his way of working, a less severely restrained expression of eternal things and of the fundamental truths behind the forms of things, but there is in compensation a moved wealth of psychic or warmth of vital suggestion, a lavish delight of the beauty of the play of the eternal in the moments of time and there the artist arrests it for us and makes moments of the life of the soul reflected in form of man or creature or incident or scene or nature full of a permanent and opulent significance to our spiritual vision. The art of the painter justifies visually to the spirit the search of the sense for delight by making it its own search for the pure intensities of meaning of the universal beauty it has revealed or hidden in creation; the indulgence of the eye's desire in perfection of form and colour becomes an enlightenment of the inner being through the power of a certain spiritually aesthetic Ananda.

Is it not a fact that the Moghul school of painting introduces a foreign element in the native spirit and tradition of Indian painting?

It has been doubted whether the Moghul paintings have anything to do with the tradition of the indigenous Indian art and are not rather an exotic importation from Persia. Almost all oriental art is akin in this respect that the psychic enters into and for the most part lays its subtler law on the physical vision and the psychic line and significance give the characteristic turn, are the secret of the decorative skill, direct the higher art in its principal motive. But there is a difference between the Persian psychicality which is redolent of the magic of the middle worlds and the Indian which is only a means of transmission of the spiritual vision. And obviously the Indo-Persian style is of the former kind and not indigenous to India. But the Moghul school is not an exotic; there is rather a blending of two mentalities: on the one side there is a leaning to some kind of externalism which is not the same thing as western naturalism, a secular spirit and certain prominent elements that are more strongly illustrative than interpretative, but the central thing is still the domination of a transforming touch which shows that there as in the architecture the Indian mind has taken hold of another invading mentality and made it a help to a more outward-going self-expression that comes in as a new strain in the spiritual continuity of achievement which began in prehistoric times and ended only with the general decline of Indian culture.

XVI

ART AND MORALITY

A number of thinkers, both ancient and modern, attach considerable importance to the purifying effect of art. Aristotle, for example, speaks of the purifying effect of tragic poetry. Does art exercise such a purifying influence?

Aristotle assigns a high value to tragedy because of its purifying force. He describes its effect as *katharsis,* a sacramental word of the Greek mysteries, which, in the secret discipline of the ancient Greek Tantrics, answered precisely to our *cittaśuddhi,* the purification of the *citta* or mass of established ideas, feelings and actional habits in a man either by *saṁyama,* rejection, or by *bhoga,* satisfaction, or by both. Aristotle was speaking of the purification of feelings, passions and emotions in the heart through imaginative treatment in poetry but the truth the idea contains is of much wider application and constitutes the justification of the aesthetic side of art.

How is this purifying effect produced by the aesthetic side of art? What is its value in life?

It purifies by beauty. It raises and purifies conduct by instilling a distaste for the coarse desires and passions of the savage, for the rough, uncouth and excessive in action and manner, and restraining both feeling and action by a striving after the decent, the beautiful, the fit and seemly which received its highest expression in the manners of cultivated European society, the elaborate ceremonious life of the Confucian, the careful *ācāra* and etiquette of Hinduism. At the present stage of progress this element is losing much of its once all-important value and, when overstressed, tends to hamper a higher development by the obstruction of soulless ceremony and formalism. Its great use was to discipline the savage animal instincts of the body, the vital instincts and the lower feelings in the heart. Its disadvantage to progress is that it tends to trammel the play both of the higher feelings of the heart and the workings of originality in thought. Born originally of a seeking after beauty, it degenerates into an attachment to form, to exterior uniformity, to precedent, to dead authority. In the future development of humanity it must be given a much lower place than in the past. Its limits must be recognised and the demands of a higher truth, sincerity and freedom of thought and feeling must be given priority. Mankind is apt to bind itself by attachment to the means of its past progress forgetful of the aim. The bondage to formulas has to be outgrown, and in this again it is the sense of a higher beauty and fitness which will be most powerful to correct the lower. The art of life must be understood in more magnificent terms and must subordinate its more formal elements to the service of the master civilisers, Love and Thought.

Does this aesthetic sense serve no higher purpose than merely refining the external conduct of man?

A still more important and indispensable activity of the sense of beauty is the powerful help it has given to the formation of morality. We do not ordinarily recognise how largely our sense of virtue is a sense of the beautiful in conduct and our sense of sin a sense of ugliness and deformity in conduct. It may easily be recognised in the lower and more physical workings, as for instance in the shuddering recoil from cruelty, blood-thirst, torture as things intolerably hideous to sight and imagination or in the aesthetic disgust at sensual excesses and the strong sense, awakened by this disgust, of the charm of purity and the beauty of virginity. This latter feeling was extremely active in the imagination of the Greeks and other nations not noted for a high standard in conduct, and it was purely aesthetic in its roots. Pity again is largely a vital instinct in the ordinary man associated with *jugupsā*, the loathing for the hideousness of its opposite, *ghṛṇā,* disgust at the sordidness and brutality of cruelty, hardness and selfishness as well as at the ugliness of their actions, so that a common word for cruel in the Sanskrit language is *nirghṛṇā*, the man without disgust or loathing, and the word *ghṛṇā* approximates in use to *kṛpā*, the lower or vital kind of pity. But even on a higher plane the sense of virtue is very largely aesthetic and, even when it emerges from the aesthetic stage, must always call the sense of the beautiful to its support if it is to be safe from the revolt against it of one of the most deep-seated of human instincts. We can see the largeness of this element if we study the ideas of the Greeks, who never got beyond the aesthetic stage of morality. There were four gradations in Greek ethical thought, — the *euprepees*, that which is seemly or outwardly decorous; the *dikaion*, that which is in accordance with *dikē* or *nomos*, the law, custom and standard of humanity based on the sense of fitness and on the codified or uncodified mass of precedents in which that sense has been expressed in general conduct, — in other words the just or lawful; thirdly, the *agathon*, the good, based partly on the seemly and partly on the just and lawful, and reaching towards the purely beautiful; then final and supreme, the *kalon*, that which is purely beautiful, the supreme standard. The most remarkable part of Aristotle's moral system is that in which he classifies the parts of conduct not according to our idea of virtue and sin, *pāpa* amd *puṇya*, but by a purely aesthetic standard, the excess, defect and golden, in other words correct and beautiful, mean of qualities.

Can this aesthetic standard of the Greeks be considered to be the sufficient standard of morality?

The Greeks' view of life was imperfect even from the standpoint of beauty, not only because the idea of beauty was not sufficiently catholic and too much attached to a fastidious purity of form and outline and restraint, but because they were deficient in love. God as beauty, Sri Krishna in Brindavan, *Śyāmsundara*, is not only Beauty, He is also Love, and without perfect love there cannot be perfect beauty, and without perfect beauty there cannot be perfect delight. The aesthetic motive in conduct limits and must be exceeded in order that humanity may rise. Therefore it was that the Greek mould had to be broken and humanity even revolted for a time against beauty. The excess of this anti-aesthetic tendency is visible in Puritanism and the baser forms of asceticism. The progress of ethics in Europe has been largely a struggle between the Greek sense of aesthetic beauty and the Christian sense of a higher good marred on the one side by formalism, on the other by an unlovely asceticism. The association of the latter with virtue has largely driven the sense of beauty to the side of vice.

What is then the true relation between the aesthetic sense of beauty and the moral sense of good?

The good must not be subordinated to the aesthetic sense, but it must be beautiful and delightful, or to that extent it ceases to be good. The object of existence is not the practice of virtue for its own sake but *ānanda*, delight, and progress consists not in rejecting beauty and delight, but in rising from the lower to the higher, the less complete to the more complete beauty and to delight.

Many thinkers consider the beautiful and the good to be the same. How far is this idea true?

Though the idea may be wrongly stated, it is when put from the right standpoint, not only a truth but the fundamental truth of existence. According to our own philosophy the whole world came out of *ānanda* and returns into *ānanda*, and the triple term in which *ānanda* may be stated is Joy, Love, Beauty. To see divine beauty in the whole world, man, life, nature, to love that which we have seen and to have pure unalloyed bliss in that love and that beauty is the appointed road by which mankind as a race must climb to God. That is the reaching to *vidyā* through *avidyā*, to the One Pure and Divine through the manifold manifestation of Him, of which the Upanishad repeatedly speaks. But the bliss must be pure and unalloyed, unalloyed by self-regarding emotions, unalloyed by pain and evil. The sense of good and bad, beautiful and un-beautiful, which afflicts our understanding and our senses, must be replaced by *akhaṇḍa rasa*, undifferentiated and unabridged delight in the delightfulness of things, before the highest can be reached. On the way to this goal full use must be made of the lower and abridged sense of beauty which seeks to replace the less beautiful by the more, the lower by the higher, the mean by the noble.

Tagore in one of his essays says: "The good is necessarily beautiful. Beauty is the picture of the good, goodness is the reality behind beauty." Is this true?

These epigrammatic sentences are difficult to understand. The divine good is no doubt necessarily beautiful, hence on a higher plane good and beauty and all else that is divine in origin meet, coalesce, harmonise. But what men call good is often ugly or drab or unattractive. Hence beauty is not always the picture of the good, it is sometimes the mask of evil — the reality behind that mask is not always goodness. These things are obvious, but probably Rabindranath meant good and beauty in their higher aspects or their essence.

XVII

ART AND NATIONAL CHARACTER — POETRY, MUSIC AND ART

Is the psychological character and actual life of a nation in any way influenced or determined by the artistic sense of its people?

The manners, the social culture and the restraint in action and expression which are so large a part of national prestige and dignity and make a nation admired like the French, loved like the Irish or respected like the higher-class English, is based essentially on the sense of form and beauty, of what is correct, symmetrical, well-adjusted, fair to the eye and pleasing to the imagination. The absence of these qualities is a source of national weakness. The rudeness, coarseness and vulgar violence of the less cultured Englishman, the over-bearing brusqueness and selfishness of the Prussian have greatly hampered those powerful nations in their dealings with foreigners, dependencies and even their own friends, allies, colonies. We all know what a large share the manner and ordinary conduct of the average and of the vulgar Anglo-Indian has had in bringing about the revolt of the Indian, accustomed through ages to courtesy, dignity and the amenities of an equal intercourse, against the mastery of an obviously coarse and selfish community. Now the sense of form and beauty, the correct, symmetrical, well-adjusted, fair and pleasing is an artistic sense and can best be fostered in a nation by artistic culture of the perceptions and sensibilities. It is noteworthy that the two great nations who are most hampered by the defect of these qualities in action are also the least imaginative, poetic and artistic in Europe. It is the South German who contributes the art, poetry and music of Germany, the Celt and Norman who produce great poets and a few great artists in England without altering the characteristics of the dominant Saxon. Music is even more powerful in this direction than Art and by the perfect expression of harmony insensibly steeps the man in it. And it is noticeable that England has hardly produced a single musician worth the name. Plato in his Republic has dwelt with extraordinary emphasis on the importance of music in education; as is the music to which a people is accustomed, so, he says in effect, is the character of that people. The importance of painting and sculpture is hardly less. The mind is profoundly influenced by what it sees and, if the eye is trained from the days of childhood to the contemplation and understanding of beauty, harmony and just arrangement in line and colour, the tastes, habits and character will be insensibly trained to follow a similar law of beauty, harmony and just arrangement in the life of the adult man. This was the great importance of the universal proficiency in the arts and crafts or the appreciation of them, which was prevalent in ancient Greece, in certain European ages, in Japan and in the better days of our own history. Art galleries cannot be brought into every home, but, if all the appointments of our life and furniture of our homes are things of taste and beauty, it is inevitable that the habits, thoughts and feelings of the people should be raised, ennobled, harmonised, made more sweet and dignified.

Is there any difference in the ways in which poetry, music and the arts of painting and sculpture exercise their influence on our life and character?

The purification of the heart, the *cittassuddhi,* which Aristotle assigned as the essential office of poetry is done in poetry by the detached and disinterested enjoyment of the eight *rasas* or forms of emotional aestheticism which make up life unalloyed by the disturbance of the lower self-regarding passions. Painting and sculpture work in the same direction by different means. Art sometimes uses the same means as poetry but cannot do it to the same extent because it has not the movement of poetry; it is fixed, still, it expresses only a given moment, a given point in space and cannot move freely through time and region. But it is precisely this stillness, this calm, this fixity which gives its separate value to Art. Poetry raises the emotions and gives each its separate delight. Art stills the emotions and teaches them the delight of a restrained and limited satisfaction, — this indeed was the characteristic that the Greeks, a nation of artists far more artistic than poetic, tried to bring into their poetry. Music deepens the emotions and harmonises them with each other. Between them music, art and poetry are a perfect education for the soul, they make and keep its movements purified, self-controlled, deep and harmonious. These, therefore, are agents which cannot profitably be neglected by humanity on its onward march or degraded to the mere satisfaction of sensuous pleasure which will disintegrate rather than build the character. They are, when properly used, great educating, edifying and civilising forces.

Some persons consider music to be far superior in its aesthetic appeal to poetry or the arts of painting and sculpture. Is this really so?

Is it necessary to fix a scale of greatness between two fine arts when each has its own greatness and can touch in its own way the extremes of aesthetic Ananda? Music, no doubt, goes nearest to the infinite and to the essence of things because it relies wholly on the ethereal vehicle, *śabda*, (architecture by the by can do something of the same kind at the other extreme even in its imprisonment in mass); but painting and sculpture have their revenge by liberating visible form into ecstasy, while poetry though it cannot do with sound what music does, yet can make a many-stringed harmony, a sound revelation winging the creation by the word and setting afloat vivid suggestion of form and colour, — that gives it in a very subtle kind the power of all the arts. Who shall decide between such claims or be a judge between these godheads?

Some people differentiate poetry from music by saying that poetry is to be mentally understood while music is to be felt and experienced. Is this true?

The difference is not that poetry has to be understood and music or singing has to be felt (*anubhūti*); that one has to reach the soul through the precise written sense and the other through the suggestion of sound and its appeal to some inner chord within us. If you only understand the intellectual content of a poem, its words and ideas, you have not really appreciated the poem at all, and a poem which contains only that and nothing else, is not true poetry. A true poem contains something more which has to be felt just as you feel music and that is its more important and essential part. Poetry has a rhythm, just as music has, though of a different kind, and it is the rhythm that helps this something else to come out through the medium of the words. The words by themselves do not carry it or cannot bring it out altogether, and this is shown by the fact that the same words written in a different order and without rhythm or without the proper rhythm would not at all move or impress you in the same way. This something else is an inner content or suggestion, a soul-feeling or soul-experience, a life-feeling or life-experience, a mental emotion, vision or experience, (not merely an idea), and it is only when you can catch this and reproduce some vibration of the experience — if not the experience itself — in you that you have got what the poem can give you, not otherwise.

What then is the real difference between poetry and music or between a poem and a song?

The real difference between a poem and a song is that a song is written with a view to be set to musical rhythm and a poem is written with the ear listening for the needed poetic rhythm or word-music. These two rhythms are quite different. That is why a poem cannot be set to music unless it has either been written with an eye to both kinds of rhythm or else happens to have (without especially intending it) a movement which makes it easy or at least possible to set it to music. This happens often with lyrical poetry, less often with other kinds. There is also this usual character of a song that it is satisfied to be very simple in its content, just bringing out an idea or feeling, and leaving it to the music to develop its unspoken values. Still this reticence is not always observed; the word claims for itself sometimes a larger importance.

> *In countries influenced by the democratic, socialistic or communistic ideology which insists on bringing down art to the level of the common people, popular verse and folk-songs are claimed to be of greater cultural value than poetry and music which require a developed taste for appreciation. Is this claim valid?*

Popular verse catches the child ear or the common ear much more easily than the music of developed poetry because it relies on a crude jingle or infantile lilt — not because it enshrines in its movements the true native spirit of the chant. It is a fallacy to think that the real spirit and native movement of a language can be caught only in crude and primitive forms and that it is disguised in the more perfect work in which it has developed its own possibilities to their full pitch, variety and scope. It is as if one maintained that the true note and fundamental nature of the evolving soul were to be sought in the earthworm or the scarabaeus and not in the developed human being — or in the divinised man or Jivanmukta.

XVIII

INTELLECTUAL AND SPIRITUAL VALUE OF ART

Since the aim of Art is to reveal beauty and yield delight, it is maintained that it can be of no use in the training and development of our intellectual faculty which is concerned with the seeking of rational truth. Is this true?

Our intellectual activity has a double character divided between the imaginative, creative and sympathetic or comprehensive intellectual centres on the one side and the critical, analytic and penetrative on the other. The latter are best trained by science, criticism and observation; the former by art, poetry, music, literature and the sympathetic study of man and his creations. These make the mind quick to grasp at a glance, subtle to distinguish shades, deep to reject shallow self-sufficiency, mobile, delicate, swift, intuitive. Art assists in this training by raising images in the mind which it has to understand not by analysis, but by self-identification with other minds; it is a powerful stimulator of sympathetic insight. Art is subtle and delicate, and it makes the mind also in its movements subtle and delicate. It is suggestive, and the intellect habituated to the appreciation of art is quick to catch suggestions, mastering not only, as the scientific mind does, that which is positive and on the surface, but that which leads to ever fresh widening and subtilising of knowledge and opens a door into the deeper secrets of inner nature where the positive instruments of science cannot take the depth or measure. This supreme intellectual value of Art has never been sufficiently recognised. Men have made language, poetry, history, philosophy agents for the training of this side of intellectuality, necessary parts of a liberal education, but the immense educative force of music, painting and sculpture has not been duly recognised. They have been thought to be by-paths of the human mind, beautiful and interesting, but not necessary, therefore intended for the few. Yet the universal impulse to enjoy the beauty and attractiveness of sound, to look at and live among pictures, colours, forms ought to have warned mankind of the superficiality and ignorance of such a view of these eternal and important occupations of the human mind. The impulse, denied proper training and self-purification, has spent itself on the trivial, gaudy, sensuous, cheap or vulgar instead of helping man upward by its powerful aid in the evocation of what is best and highest in intellect as well as in character, emotion and the aesthetic enjoyment and regulation of life and manners. It is difficult to appreciate the waste and detriment involved in the low and debased level of enjoyment to which the artistic impulses are condemned in the majority of mankind.

Beyond the intellect is the spirit; can Art be of any help in the discovery and expression of the spirit in life which is the highest of all human endeavours?

Beyond and above this intellectual utility of Art, there is a higher use, the noblest of all, its service to the growth of spirituality in the race. European critics have dwelt on the close connection of the highest developments of art with religion, and it is undoubtedly true that in Greece, in Italy, in India, the greatest efflorescence of a national Art has been associated with the employment of the artistic genius to illustrate or adorn the thoughts and fancies or the temples and instruments of the national religion. This was not because Art is necessarily associated with the outward forms of religion, but because it was in the religion that men's spiritual aspirations centred themselves. Spirituality is a wider thing than formal religion and it is in the service of spirituality that Art reaches its highest self-expression. Spirituality is a single word expressive of three lines of human aspiration: towards divine knowledge, divine love and joy, divine strength, and that will be the highest and most perfect Art which, while satisfying the physical requirements of the aesthetic sense, the laws of formal beauty, the emotional demand of humanity, the portrayal of life and outward reality, as the best European Art satisfies these requirements, reaches beyond them and expresses inner spiritual truth, the deeper not obvious reality of things, the joy of God in the world and its beauty and desirableness and the manifestation of divine force and energy in phenomenal creation. This is what Indian Art alone attempted thoroughly and in the effort it often dispensed, either deliberately or from impatience, with the lower, yet not negligible perfections which the more material European demanded. Therefore Art has flowed in two separate streams in Europe and Asia, so diverse that it is only now that the European aesthetic sense has so far trained itself as to begin to appreciate the artistic conventions, aims and traditions of Asia. Asia's future development will unite these two streams in one deep and grandiose flood of artistic self-expression perfecting the aesthetic evolution of humanity.

But can Art, which even at its highest is an activity of the limited human mind, possibly express the eternal and infinite Truth, Love, Joy and Power of the Spirit?

Art can express eternal truth, it is not limited to the expression of form and appearance. So wonderfully has God made the world that a man using a simple combination of lines, an unpretentious harmony of colours, can raise this apparently insignificant medium to suggest absolute and profound truths with a perfection which language labours with difficulty to reach. What Nature is, what God is, what man is can be triumphantly revealed in stone or on canvas.

Behind a few figures, a few trees and rocks, the supreme Intelligence, the supreme Imagination, the supreme Energy lurks, acts, feels, is, and, if the artist has the spiritual vision, he can see it and suggest perfectly the great mysterious Life in its manifestations brooding in action, active in thought, energetic in stillness, creative in repose, full of a mastering intention in that which appears blind and unconscious. The great truths of religion, science, metaphysics, life, development, become concrete, emotional, universally intelligible and convincing in the hands of the master of plastic Art, and the soul of man, in the stage when it is rising from emotion to intellect, looks, receives the suggestion and is uplifted towards a higher development, a diviner knowledge.

So it is with the divine love and joy which pulsates throughout existence and is far superior to alloyed earthly pleasure. Catholic, perfect, unmixed with repulsion, radiating through all things, the common no less than the high, the mean and shabby no less than the lofty and splendid, the terrible and the repulsive no less than the charming and attractive, it uplifts all, purifies all, turns all to love and delight and beauty. A little of this immortal nectar poured into man's heart transfigures life and action. The whole flood of it pouring in would lift mankind to God. This too Art can seize on and suggest to the human soul, aiding it in its stormy and toilsome pilgrimage. In that pilgrimage it is the divine strength that supports. *Śakti,* Force, pouring through the universe supports its boundless activities, the frail and tremulous life of the rose no less than the flaming motions of sun and star. To suggest the strength and virile unconquerable force of the divine Nature in man and in the outside world, its energy, its calm, its powerful inspiration, its august enthusiasm, its wildness, greatness, attractiveness, to breathe that into man's soul and gradually mould the finite into the image of the Infnite is another spiritual utility of Art. This is its loftiest function, its fullest consummation, its most perfect privilege.

APPENDIX

REFERENCES

In all the sections of the two Series in this book the questions are framed by the compiler and the answers to them consist of appropriate passages directly reproduced from different works of Sri Aurobindo. The references to Sri Aurobindo's works from which the answers are taken are shown with the answers in the list below. The answers in the list are serially numbered for each section, but as they are not numbered in the book, corresponding page numbers are given in brackets along with each answer.

All the references given in the list are from the Centenary Edition of Sri Aurobindo's works published in 30 volumes in Sri Aurobindo Birth Centenary Library. In each reference the Centenary Edition is abbreviated as C.E. and shown in brackets with the relevant volume number of the work from which the reference is taken.

As stated in the Compiler's Note at the beginning of the book, the text of the passages quoted in some of the answers is not exactly similar to the original text in Sri Aurobindo's works because Sri Aurobindo himself made alterations in them before approving them for publication in *Mother India*. Some of these alterations were of a minor nature but some others were quite extensive. Especially in the earlier sections of the First Series the alterations made by him are often elaborate, with the result that the dissimilarity between the passages quoted in the answers and the original text is considerable. Also at some places minor verbal changes were made at the beginning of the passages quoted in the answers to suit them exactly to the preceding questions. These were seen by Sri Aurobindo before giving approval. Also in some cases, where the passages quoted in the answers were taken from Sri Aurobindo's articles in the "Arya", they have been substituted by the same passages as later revised by him when these articles were published in book form.

In section XIII of the Second Series, dealing with Indian Architecture, a new foot-note was inserted by Sri Aurobindo at the end of the last answer. (See p. 170.)
The list of references follows:

FIRST SERIES

SECTION I

Answer	Reference
1	*Letters on Yoga* (C.E. 22), p. 467.
2	*Ibid.*
3	*Ibid.*, pp. 467-68.
4	*Ibid.*, p. 469.
5	*Ibid.*, pp. 468-69.
6	*Ibid.*, p. 468.
7	*Ibid.*
8	*Ibid.*

SECTION II

1	*Nirodbaran's Correspondence with Sri Aurobindo* (Complete Set), Vol. One, p. 482.
2	*Ibid.*, p. 483.
3	*Ibid.*, p. 484.
4	*Letters on Yoga* (C.E. 24), p. 1354.

SECTION III

1	*Letters on Yoga* (C.E. 23), pp. 756-59.
2	*Ibid.*, pp. 759-60.
3	*Ibid.*, pp. 817-18.
4	*Ibid.*, p. 756.
5	*Ibid.*, pp. 761-62.
6	*Ibid.*, p. 818.
7	*Ibid.*, p. 772.
8	*Ibid.*

SECTION IV

1	*Letters on Yoga* (C.E. 24), pp. 1519-20; *The Synthesis of Yoga* (C.E. 20) p. 203.
2	*Letters on Yoga* (C.E. 24), pp. 1516-17.
3	*Ibid.*
4	*Nirodbaran's Correspondence with Sri Aurobindo* (Complete Set), Vol. One, p. 107.

References 227

5	*Letters on Yoga* (C.E. 24), p. 1526.
6	*Ibid.*
7	*Ibid.*, pp. 1525-27.
8	*Ibid.*, pp. 1525-26.

Section V

1	*Letters on Yoga* (C.E. 24), pp. 1516-18.
2	*The Brain of India* (C.E. 3), pp. 334-35.
3	*Letters on Yoga* (C.E. 24), p. 1511.
4	*Ibid.*, p. 1606.

Section VI

1	*The Human Cycle* (C.E. 15), p. 164.
2	*Ibid.*, pp. 165-66.
3	*Ibid.*, p. 166.
4	*Ibid.*, pp. 168-70.
5	*Letters on Yoga* (C.E. 22), p. 140.

Section VII

1	*The Human Cycle* (C.E. 15), pp. 121 and 125.
2	*Ibid.*, p. 122.
3	*Ibid.*
4	*Ibid., p. 123.*
5	*Ibid.*, pp. 123-24.
6	*Ibid.*, pp. 124-25.
7	*Ibid.*, p. 126.

Section VIII

1	*Letters on Yoga* (C.E. 22), pp. 226-27.
2	*Ibid.*, pp. 228-29.
3	*The Life Divine* (C.E. 19), pp. 874-75.
4	*Ibid.*, p. 876.
5	*Ibid.*, pp. 876-77.
6	*Ibid.*

Section IX

1	*Letters on Yoga* (C.E. 22), p. 85.
2	*Ibid.*
3	*Ibid.*, pp. 445-48.
4	*Ibid.*, p. 486.
5	*Ibid.*
6	*Ibid.*

7	*Ibid.*
8	*Ibid.*, pp. 159-60.
9	*Ibid.*, p. 459.
10	*Ibid.*, pp. 214-25.

SECTION X

1	*The Synthesis of Yoga* (C.E. 20), pp. 191-92.
2	*Ibid.*, p. 192.
3	*The Human Cycle* (C.E. 15), p. 138; *The Synthesis of Yoga* (C.E. 20), pp. 188-89.
4	*Ibid.*, pp. 189-91.
5	*The Human Cycle* (C.E. 15), pp. 139-40.

SECTION XI

1	*The Human Cycle* (C.E. 15), p. 146.
2	*The Synthesis of Yoga* (C.E. 20), p. 183; *The Human Cycle* (C.E. 15), p. 141.
3	*The Human Cycle* (C.E. 15), p. 142.
4	*Ibid.*
5	*Ibid.*, p. 143.
6	*Ibid.*, pp. 143-44.

SECTION XII

1	*The Problem of Rebirth* (C.E. 16), p. 202.
2	*Ibid.*, pp. 202-203.
3	*Ibid.*, p. 203.
4	*Ibid.*, pp. 203-204.
5	*Ibid.*, pp. 199-200.
6	*Ibid.*, p. 200.
7	*Ibid.*
8	*Ibid.*, p. 201.

SECTION XIII

1	*The Problem of Rebirth* (C.E. 16), p. 125.
2	*Ibid.*, p. 126.
3	*The Life Divine* (C.E. 19), pp. 807-808.
4	*Ibid.*, pp. 127-29.
5	*Ibid.*, p. 176.
6	*Letters on Yoga* (C.E. 22), p. 493.

SECTION XIV

1	*The Problem of Rebirth* (C.E. 16), pp. 138-39.

2	*Ibid.*, p. 135.
3	*Ibid.*, pp. 141-42.
4	*Ibid.*, p. 142.
5	*Ibid.*, pp. 142-43.

SECTION XV

1	*The Problem of Rebirth* (C.E. 16), p. 153.
2	*Ibid.*, pp. 153-54.
3	*Ibid.*, p. 154.
4	*Ibid.*, pp. 154-55.
5	*Ibid.*, pp. 155-56.
6	*Ibid.*, pp. 156-57.
7	*Ibid.*, pp. 160-61.

SECTION XVI

1	*The Life Divine* (C.E. 19), pp. 805-06.
2	*Ibid.*, pp. 808-09.
3	*Ibid.*, pp. 811-12.
4	*Ibid.*, pp. 813-14.
5	*Ibid.*, pp. 814-16.

SECTION XVII

1	*The Problem of Rebirth* (C.E. 16), pp. 209-210.
2	*Ibid.*, p. 210.
3	*Ibid.*, p. 211.
4	*Ibid.*, pp. 211-12.
5	*Ibid.*, pp. 212-13.

SECTION XVIII

1	*The Problem of Rebirth* (C.E. 16), pp. 216-17.
2	*Ibid.*, pp. 217-18.
3	*Ibid.*, pp. 218-19.
4	*Ibid.*, p. 219.
5	*Ibid.*, p. 216.
6	*Ibid.*, pp. 219-20.

SECTION XIX

1	*The Human Cycle* (C.E. 15), pp. 50-51.
2	*Ibid.*, pp. 51-52.
3	*Ibid.*, pp. 53-55.

SECTION XX

1	*The Human Cycle* (C.E. 15), p. 235.

Section XXI

2	*Ibid.*, pp. 235-36.
3	*Ibid.*, pp. 236-37.
4	*Ibid.*, pp. 237-39.
5	*Ibid.*, pp. 237-38.

Section XXI

1	*The Human Cycle* (C.E. 15), pp. 23-24.
2	*Ibid.*, p. 24.
3	*Ibid.*, pp. 25-26.
4	*Ibid.*, p. 27.
5	*Ibid.*, pp. 27-28.

Section XXII

1	*The Life Divine* (C.E. 19), pp. 1027-29.
2	*Letters on Poetry, Literature and Art* (C.E. 9), pp. 555-56.
3	*The Life Divine* (C.E. 19), p. 649.
4	*Ibid.*, pp. 649-51.

Section XXIII

1	*The Life Divine* (C.E. 19), p. 644.
2	*Ibid.*, (C.E. 19), p. 645; (C.E. 18), p. 119.
3	*Ibid.*, (C.E. 18), p. 118; (C.E. 19) p. 646.
4	*Ibid.*, (C.E. 19), p. 645.

Section XXIV

1	*Evolution,* "Materialism" (C.E. 16), pp. 245-46.
2	*Ibid.*, pp. 246-47.
3	*Ibid.*, pp. 247-48.
4	*Ibid.*, pp. 248-49.
5	*Ibid.*, p. 249.
6	*Ibid.*, p. 249-50.
7	*Ibid.*, p. 250.
8	*Ibid.*, pp. 250-51.

Section XXV

1	*Evolution,* "Materialism" (C.E. 16), p. 251.
2	*Ibid.*, p. 252.
3	*Ibid.*, pp. 252-53.
4	*Ibid.*, pp. 253-54.
5	*Ibid.*, pp. 254-56.
6	*Ibid.*, p. 256.

References

SECOND SERIES

Section I

Answer	Reference
1	*Letters on Poetry, Literature and Art* (C.E. 9), pp. 330-31.
2	*Ibid.*, p. 331.
3	*Ibid.*, pp. 331-32.
4	*Ibid.*, pp. 332-33.
5	*Ibid.*, p. 333.
6	*Ibid.*, pp. 333-34.
7	*Ibid.*, pp. 334-35.

Section II

1	*Letters on Poetry, Literature and Art* (C.E. 9), pp. 31 and 33.
2	*Ibid.*, pp. 31-32.
3	*Ibid.*, p. 33.
4	*Ibid.*, pp. 320-21; *Savitri* (C.E. 29), p. 737.

Section III

1	*Letters on Poetry, Literature and Art* (C.E 9), p. 212.
2	*Ibid.*, p. 212.
3	*Ibid.*, pp. 213-14.
4	*Ibid.*, pp. 214-16.

Section IV

1	*Letters on Poetry, Literature and Art* (C.E.9), pp. 227-28.
2	*Ibid.*, p. 193.
3	*Ibid.*, p. 195.
4	*Ibid.*, pp. 228-29.

Section V

1	*Letters on Poetry, Literature and Art* (C.E. 9), p. 230.
2	*Ibid.*, p. 230.
3	*Ibid.*, p. 231.
4	*Ibid.*
5	*Ibid.*
6	*Ibid.*, pp. 232-33
7	*Ibid.*, p. 233.

Section VI

1	*Letters on Poetry, Literature and Art* (C.E. 9), pp. 454 and 197.
2	*Ibid.*, p. 194.
3	*Ibid.*, p. 193.
4	*Ibid.*, p. 227.
5	*Ibid.*, pp. 195-97

Section VII

1	*Letters on Poetry, Literature and Art* (C.E. 9), p. 537.
2	*Ibid.*, pp. 537-38.
3	*Ibid.*, p. 538.
4	*Ibid.*, p. 445.
5	*Ibid.*, pp. 446-47.

Section VIII

1	*Letters on Poetry, Literature and Art* (C.E. 9), pp. 447-48.
2	*The Life Divine* (C.E. 18), p. 424.
3	*Ibid.*, pp. 422-23 and 425-26.
4	*Letters on Poetry, Literature and Art* (C.E. 9), p. 448.

Section IX

1	*Letters on Poetry, Literature and Art* (C.E. 9), p. 473.
2	*Ibid.*, p. 471.
3	*Ibid.*
4	*Ibid.*, p. 472.
5	*Ibid.*

Section X

1	*Letters on Poetry, Literature and Art* (C.E. 9), pp. 38 and 42-43.
2	*Ibid.*, pp. 38-39.
3	*Ibid.*, pp. 39-40.
4	*Ibid.*, p. 40.
5	*Ibid.*

Section XI

1	*The Foundations of Indian Culture* (C.E. 14), pp. 200 and 205-206.
2	*Ibid.*, pp. 207-208.
3	*Ibid.*, p. 208
4	*Ibid.*

References

5	*Ibid.*, pp. 208-209.
6	*Ibid.*, pp. 209-210.

SECTION XII

1	*The Foundations of Indian Culture* (C.E. 14), pp. 211-13.
2	*Ibid.*, pp. 213-14.
3	*Ibid.*, pp. 216-17.
4	*Ibid.*, pp. 219-20.

SECTION XIII

1	*The Foundations of Indian Culture* (C.E. 14), pp. 220-21.
2	*Ibid.*, p. 221.
3	*Ibid.*, pp. 221-23.
4	*Ibid.*, pp. 224-25.
5	*Reviews*, "Rupam" (C.E. 17), p. 303.

SECTION XIV

1	*The Foundations of Indian Culture* (C.E. 14), pp. 228-29.
2	*Ibid.*, pp. 229-31.
3	*Ibid.*, pp. 229-30.
4	*Ibid.*, pp. 231-32.
5	*Ibid.*, pp. 237-38.

SECTION XV

1	*The Foundations of Indian Culture* (C.E. 14), pp. 239-40.
2	*Ibid.*, pp. 240-41.
3	*Ibid.*, pp. 241-42.
4	*Ibid.*, pp. 242-43.
5	*Ibid.*, p. 253.

SECTION XVI

1	*The National Value of Art* (C.E. 17), p. 237.
2	*Ibid.*, pp. 237-39.
3	*Ibid.*, pp. 240-41.
4	*Ibid.*, pp. 241-42.
5	*Ibid.*, p. 241.
6	*Ibid.*, pp. 237-38.
7	*Sri Aurobindo Circle*, 14th Number, 1958, p. 72.

SECTION XVII

1	*The National Value of Art* (C.E. 17), pp. 244-45.
2	*Ibid.*, pp. 245-46.

3	*Letters on Poetry, Literature and Art* (C.E. 9), p. 481.
4	*Ibid.*, pp. 423-24.
5	*Ibid.*, p. 424.
6	*Ibid.*, pp. 422-23.

SECTION XVIII

1	*The National Value of Art* (C.E. 17), pp. 247-48.
2	*Ibid.*, pp. 248-49.
3	*Ibid.*, pp. 249-50.